It Comes with the Territory

It Comes with the Territory

Handling Problem Situations in Libraries

by
ANNE M. TURNER

with a foreword by
GORDON M. CONABLE

McFarland & Company, Inc., Publishers
Jefferson, North Carolina, and London

British Library Cataloguing-in-Publication data are available

Library of Congress Cataloguing-in-Publication Data

Turner, Anne M., 1941–
    It comes with the territory : handling problem situations in
libraries / by Anne M. Turner.
        p.   cm.
    Includes bibliographical references (p.   ) and index. ∞
    ISBN 0-89950-844-8 (lib. bdg. : 50# alk. paper)
    1. Libraries and readers.   2. Library rules and regulations.
3. Public libraries—United States.   I. Title.
Z711.T87   1993
025.5—dc20   93-255
                                                             CIP

Manufactured in the United States of America

McFarland & Company, Inc., Publishers
  Box 611, Jefferson, North Carolina 28640

To Steve, for all the love,
for all the years,
and to the staff,
past and present, of the
Santa Cruz City County Library System

Table of Contents

Foreword

(Gordon M. Conable)

The first time my job description included interviewing potential staff members, I started asking people why they wanted to work in the library. "It seems like it would be a nice quiet place to work" rapidly reached the top five responses and it began to dawn on me that a significant number of librarians and library employees were really seeking jobs that would provide them some sense of shelter from the less pleasant aspects of human interaction. A surprising number of them seemed to think this is a cloistered occupation. I was hiring public service staff and had a different set of priorities, but the attitude expressed by that response has always been present in significant numbers of the staff members of every library of any size that I've ever worked in.

Whatever their occupational motivation, many librarians shy away from potentially confrontational or difficult situations. But as with any public service, libraries get to deal with the widest imaginable range of humanity, some of whose members are dangerous, threatening, smelly, or just unpleasant. Dealing with some of them is hardly the best part of the job.

After twenty years in the public service departments of public libraries, as an administrator, and as a director, I am now much more fully aware of the astonishing range of difficult situations that confront librarians on a daily basis — situations, generated by human beings, that are complex, perplexing, and that frequently tax patience, ingenuity, and good will.

I have ducked the punches of a confused individual the size of a pick-up truck, considered the most tactful approach to the sleeping patron whose jogging shorts revealed considerably more than his lack of undergarments, worried about the woman camping in the car in the

parking lot after the library closed, confronted the peeper hiding in the
ceiling tiles over the rest room, pondered what to do about the woman
who wanted all the encyclopedia volumes arranged on the floor in
front of her before going to the index, and struggled with what to say to
the gentleman, thirty years my senior, who was misidentifying the
gender of the man in the photograph in the sex manual he was showing
me.

These are not uncommon occurrences. If you've worked in libraries for any length of time, you can surely add rich variations to this list.

At a recent American Library Association conference, during a
hearing on proposed "Guidelines for the Development of Policies
Regarding Patron Behavior and Library Usage" which grew out of the
troubles that the Morristown, New Jersey, Public Library had with a
litigious and difficult patron, I was struck by how besieged a large
number of librarians seemed to be.

My interest in the case was spurred by concerns about the
intellectual freedom issues involved — the function of the library as a
limited public forum for the receipt of information and the very right to
receive information at all — which the City of Morristown had disputed
in its legal brief in the case. But these issues were substantially less
important to many of the people present than the sense of frustration
and outrage they were expressing about the difficulty of coping with
difficult patrons and the grief which the Morristown librarians were
being put through.

Now here comes Anne Turner, a thoughtful and witty librarian,
with a lot of practical advice for the potentially beleaguered, and a darn
good book. If Anne had written this book twenty years ago, I might
have been spared a lot of grief.

It Comes with the Territory is a practical, knowledgeable guide to
dealing with behavioral problems that occur in libraries. She offers
immensely useful guidance about writing good, clear policies and
procedures. She suggests approaches to difficult problems that do not
compromise professional ethics or principles. She talks about complicated legal issues in straightforward, understandable language. In
these pages you will find support, assistance, and legal backing for
wading in and coping when angels hold back and where fools fear to
tread. There is good material here for staff training and lots of food for
thought.

The issues tackled here are crucial: handled poorly the situations
addressed in this volume can easily lead to policies, procedures, and

"solutions" that seriously compromise the library's basic mission and purpose. Efforts to address problem behaviors can lead to general approaches that interfere—however unintentionally—with the rights of all library users to free, private inquiry under safe, friendly, user-oriented conditions.

As the physician first seeks to do no harm, the librarian must first seek to impose no limits on the rights of intellectual freedom and free expression. This is all easier said than done. But Anne Turner's book should make it easier to do it well.

Gordon M. Conable is director of the Monroe County Library System, Monroe, Michigan.

Introduction and Acknowledgments

Like many of my colleagues, I found the 1991-92 library legal case popularly known as *Kreimer v. Morristown* horribly frustrating. In case you missed it, this is the one in which a public library adopted rules establishing a dress code (must wear shirts and shoes) and banning "offensive personal hygiene." A patron sued on the grounds that his First Amendment rights to information were being denied because of his homeless state (i.e., he had no place to bathe).

The patron won at the federal district court level, but the library appealed. Eventually, the federal Circuit Court judges issued what was later described as a "win-win" ruling. They made a strong statement, now embedded in case law, of the status of public libraries as "limited" public forums for free speech. But they also confirmed the people's First Amendment right to access to information.

Alas, in a statement widely quoted (and quoted approvingly) in media ranging from the *New York Times* to the editorial page of the *San Francisco Chronicle*, the judges declared, however, that libraries are places dedicated to "quiet, to knowledge and to beauty," and their purpose "is to aid in acquisition of knowledge through reading, writing, and quiet contemplation."

I am going to give the judges the benefit of the doubt, and assume that they are three old men whose last personal information acquisition experience was a daring trip down the hall to the law library at the Third Circuit Court of Appeals in Philadelphia.

They couldn't have been in a public library lately. Places dedicated to quiet and to beauty? Most of the public libraries I know are dedicated to meeting the information needs of the people. Doing the job effectively is seldom quiet and is often messy. Just take a look at the shambles around the copy machines on April 15th or the Children's Room on Story Hour days. Quiet contemplation indeed!

This disjunction between the popular perception of public libraries and the reality of library life is one of the reasons why library staffs and their governing boards have such trouble adopting and implementing fair and appropriate behavior rules. On the one hand people think of us as temples of blessed silence in a noisy world, and on the other they make demands for service which range from reference information and popular reading to shelter for street people and latchkey children.

In far too many cases, our response to this conflict has been to adopt rules which turn our libraries into fortresses, and procedures which demand that our staffs behave like police. Or, as managers, we have thrown up our hands, left our staffs alone on the desks to do the best they can, while we grumble nonsense about how "you can't even say shshhh anymore."

This book is an effort to help librarians, especially those in middle and small sized public libraries, to develop behavior rules which work, and train staffs in how to implement them with fairness and reasonable humor. It assumes that the constituency of even the smallest public library is likely to be quite varied. It also assumes that because of this, problem situations will be frequent, and that ways must be found to do the library's job anyway—delivering information services to the people.

It Comes with the Territory does not pretend to be a scholarly treatise. Rather, it tries to put together the best opinion and advice from librarians across the country, including me, based on our collective experiences. It is divided into three parts. The first two chapters are about writing behavior rules and policies for exhibits and meeting rooms in the context of recent legal cases and First Amendment law. Chapters 3 through 7 discuss each of the categories of problem behaviors with which most library staffs must deal. The final three chapters are on facilities security, writing staff manuals, and training staff.

Of course many people provided help and advice, and although I owe them a great debt for their contributions, I nevertheless take full responsibility for the opinions expressed here. I am particularly grateful to the management staff of the Santa Cruz City County Library System, of which I am the director: Susan Elgin, Gary Decker, Janis Schechter, Margaret Souza, and Fred Ulrich. They talk to me, listen to me, and together we have survived everything from earthquakes to budget cuts over the last few years. The library office staff—Barbara Wood, Ian Lawless, and Donna Paul—have also been enormously tolerant, supportive, and helpful. Librarian Mary Franich Bignell, formerly of the Santa Cruz management staff, read the whole manuscript and made many useful and incisive comments. Gordon M. Conable, president of the Freedom to Read Foundation, paused in the midst of an intellectual freedom challenge at his own library to comment on my draft and write a very nice foreword. And Ellen Pastore, the administrative and reference coordinator of the Monterey Bay Area Cooperative Library System, produced wonderful resources on demand, all the while claiming that this was what any good librarian did for any patron.

I would also like to thank the librarians, old friends and new, who allowed themselves to be interviewed (formally and informally) or made other special contributions: Rosie Brewer (Monterey Bay Area Cooperative Library System), Judith Drescher (Memphis, Tennessee), Susan Fuller (Santa Clara County, California), Carole Hildebrande (Eugene, Oregon), Bonnie Isman (Amherst, Massachusetts), Nora Jacob (Santa Ana, California), Heidi Jaeger and Barbara Kiehl (both of Santa Cruz County, California), Linda Luke (Alachua County, Florida), Mary Mahoney (Chelmsford, Massachusetts), Adrian Mixon (Alachua County, Florida), Wayne Mullin (University of California at Santa Cruz), Julia Orozco (Salinas, California), Cathy Page and Neel Parikh (both of San Francisco, California), Meredith Pierce (Alachua County, Florida), Dallas Shaffer (Monterey County, California), Beverley Simmons (Sunnyvale, California), Nancy Milnor Smith (Galveston, Texas), Pat Woodrum (Tulsa, Oklahoma), and all the library workers who attended a Santiago (California) Library System workshop on handling problem situations in October 1992.

Theresa Chmara, Esq., an associate at Jenner and Block, the law firm of Bruce Ennis, counsel to ALA's Freedom to Read Foundation, made extremely helpful comments on Chapter 1, "Making Behavior Rules." So did attorney Kate Lahey of the Utah College of Law. My thanks in this category go particularly to Santa Cruz City Attorney John Barisone: all librarians should be so lucky as to receive legal counsel from an attorney who also reads books.

Three other Santa Cruz friends were particularly helpful: Bob Smith of the Watsonville *Register Pajaronion*, Jeff Locke of the Santa Cruz Police Department, and Santa Cruz Police Chief Jack Bassett.

Finally, I am very grateful for the comments and suggestions of my father, management consultant Donald B. Tweedy, and my mother, editor Jessie M. Tweedy. Steve Turner, to whom I am married, is a professional writer, not a librarian, but you would never know it from the depth and intelligence of his comments on this manuscript and my other writing projects.

Anne M. Turner
Santa Cruz
January 1993

Part I
Writing Good Rules

1. Making Behavior Rules

Does everyone remember the old *Twilight Zone* television show in which the narrator (Rod Serling) sets the scene? *Consider this. . .a moment. . .a moment when a man, an ordinary man, goes for a drive, and. . .* I'm reminded of that preparation when I look at the library's front steps on many mornings.

> *Consider this. . .a building, a substantial building which houses books, where a woman, a once-attractive woman, now wearing a green raincoat and nothing else, waits to enter. And a man, a man carrying a bundled bedroll, also waits. A car drives up and a child climbs out. The car drives away. A person approaches the door of the building from the inside, unlocks it, holds it open. The people outside rush in.*

Who would have recognized this scene thirty years ago? Nobody but the staffs of public libraries in, say, downtown Los Angeles, New York, Boston, or St. Louis. Most people à la Norman Rockwell thought of libraries as cheerful and relatively sane places, to which citizens came to check out books, ask the odd question, and read the out-of-town newspapers. And they largely were.

But these days, the scene above is a familiar one in communities ranging from Farmington, New Mexico, to Amherst, Massachusetts. Society everywhere has changed. There are more poor people, and more mentally disabled people on the street, and more children on their own, and many of them have nowhere to go for the day but the public library. There are also many more people endeavoring to manage lives complicated by inadequate childcare resources, or a job which has disappeared, or responsibility for elderly parents, and a thousand other social and economic problems.

So they come to the library, and the staff tries to meet whatever information needs they have, while at the same time coping with the

3

special situations they create. The mess in the bathroom, made by a woman washing out her clothes. The anger of a well-dressed Friend of the Library, who is offended at the sight of the scruffy looking man in the torn jacket asleep in the magazine section. The woman who wants to check out a reference book won't take no for an answer, and tells you so in a voice which can be heard upstairs in the children's room. The kids who think the disabled access ramp is the best place in town for skateboarding. The man who likes to follow little girls around. The guy who makes photocopies of fruit, usually citrus.

None of these people, and none of these situations, would surprise the vast majority of library workers today (although some would make them laugh). It is our working reality. Our task is to do our basic job — delivering information services to all the people — in the context of a world which is vastly different from the one envisioned by those who first thought up the idea of public libraries.

As contemporary librarians we need to organize our rules for behavior, and train our staffs, so that we can cope effectively with this reality. This book is about doing that. It has four overriding themes.

The first is the most fundamental: *no one has the right to interfere with anyone else's right to use the library.* This is the premise upon which every behavior rule we make should be based. It is a simple one, and provided the rules we make to support it are equitably enforced, it is one we can stand on in any court of law.

The second theme is *that library staffs, and especially library managers, must be flexible in their approach to delivering information services in a rapidly changing world, and in devising the procedures and policies which organize how they do that.* A rule written for today may be inappropriate next year, next month, or even tomorrow. Being flexible means being willing to evaluate constantly, to throw out what is dearest to one's heart if it doesn't work, and (as a manager) to place a high value on the advice and judgment of the people who are serving the public on the front desk.

The third theme is that beyond certain minimum points, the more detailed we make our behavior rules, the more useless they are. The reason is that the people are much more creative than we are in thinking up things to do which we are not going to consider appropriate behavior in the library. Better to spend our time, and that of our staff, figuring out how to respond creatively to the unexpected. *Good procedures for handling bad situations are a whole lot more useful than good rules which don't prevent them.*

The final theme is that people are not the problem. The problem is the situations people create. *Our task is to learn how to handle problem situations, **not** problem people or problem patrons.*

It is true that we do need some rules. Among other reasons, the courts require it if we are going to impose legal sanctions on behavior which we do not regard as acceptable. We are also obligated legally to protect the staff and the property for which we are responsible.

The balance of this chapter is therefore about the legal and other bases which must be used in formulating these rules. Chapter 2 deals with the writing of policies in two other areas which flow from the same structure of law: exhibit and display policies, and use of meeting rooms.

The appendices include two documents of primary importance to discussions of these issues: the American Library Association *Library Bill of Rights*, and "Guidelines for the Development of Policies Regarding Patron Behavior and Library Usage," developed by ALA's Intellectual Freedom Committee.

An important disclaimer must be emphasized. I am not an attorney, and I do not claim to be giving any librarian legal advice. My purpose is to sort out and put into readable language all the conflicting information which has been visited on us over the last several years. Two attorneys have reviewed and made suggestions about this chapter. I believe it to be an accurate portrayal of the law as it is currently interpreted by the courts. But any library board and staff must rely on their own legal counsel for definitive advice.

The First Amendment

There are three basic sources underpinning behavior rules in libraries: the Constitution of the United States, state law and local ordinances, and local custom and culture. We begin with the Constitution, since it rightfully takes precedence over both of the other two.

> Congress shall make no law respecting an establishment of religion, or prohibiting the free exercise thereof; or abridging the freedom of speech, or of the press; or of the right of the people peaceably to assemble, and to petition the Government for redress of grievances.

This is the First Amendment of the Constitution, and the crucial phrase for our purposes is the one about "abridging the freedom of speech."

The most recent statement of the specific applicability to public libraries of the requirements of the First Amendment was in the Third Circuit Court of Appeals 1992 ruling in the case which is popularly called *Kreimer v. Morristown*.[1] In this case, the judges ruled that the Morristown public library was a "limited" public forum, that its behavior rules did *not* violate First Amendment nor due process nor equal protection clauses of the Constitution, and that its rules were not void because they were vague.

The judges' opinion reviews a series of relevant Supreme Court cases, concluding that the First Amendment "does not merely prohibit the government from enacting laws that censor information, but additionally encompasses the positive right of public access to information and ideas." While this right may not necessarily be unfettered, it does include the right to some level of access to a public library, "the quintessential locus of the receipt of information."[2]

This basic First Amendment principle is a fundamental guide for the development of behavior rules: part of any person's basic right to free speech is a right of access to information and ideas, including access to a public library.

The concept is simple enough. From here on, however, the legal issues get more complicated, because before the legitimacy of any particular rules can be decided, it is necessary to establish whether the library is a public forum for free speech, and what kind of public forum it is. That determination, never a simple one, has been made even more complicated by a Supreme Court ruling in June of 1992 involving the Hare Krishnas and the airports controlled by the New York Port Authority.[3]

In 1983 (in *Perry Education Association v. Perry Local Educators' Association*),[4] the Supreme Court identified three kinds of government fora, as attorneys call them (most people say "forums"). The definitions are important, because they determine the stringency of the rules or regulations which may be established to govern them.

The first kind of public forum is a public space, such as a park, street, or sidewalk, which has traditionally been used, from time immemorial, for public assembly, discussing public issues, etc. Not surprisingly, this is called a "traditional public forum."

The second type is public property which the government has opened for use by the people as a place for free speech. This is called a "designated public forum." A municipal auditorium is one example, and, as it turns out, so is a public library. The implication of the government "designating" a public forum is that it could, theoretically at any rate, *un*-designate it. Also, if the government has the power to make something a public forum, doesn't it therefore also have the power to say what kind of expressive acts can take place in it? These are issues which have not been fully resolved by recent litigation.

The third category includes government property, such as a communications network, which is not traditionally used by the public, and may thus be regulated, but must nevertheless meet certain First Amendment requirements.

In *Kreimer v. Morristown* the Court concluded that while the public library may be the "quintessential" locus for the exercise of free speech, it is not a traditional public forum. The reason is that people engaged in free speech and other traditional activities "would disrupt the quiet and peaceful library environment." [5]

Rather, the Court decided that a library is more like a "designated public forum," and within that category, belongs to a subgroup it created called "limited public fora" — in which "constitutional protection is afforded only to expressive activity of a genre similar to those that government has admitted to the limited forum." In other words,

> . . . the Library is obligated only to permit the public to exercise rights that are consistent with the nature of the Library and consistent with the government's intent in designating the Library as a public forum. [6]

Because the people have a right to hear and receive information and ideas, and because public libraries are a limited forum in which the people may exercise this right, any rules which libraries adopt are subject to what attorneys call "heightened scrutiny." That is, they will be more carefully examined to make sure they meet a higher standard of fairness than they would be if the library were not a public forum. And the courts have traditionally applied various tests for determining whether or not they do.

Attorney Kate Lahey, who is a trustee of the Salt Lake City Library, and a professor at the Utah College of Law, gives a useful summary of the tests the courts have established which library rules must pass if they are to meet First Amendment requirements. [7] She points out that while the tests are organized into three parts for purposes of clarity, in fact they are mutually dependent, and should not be considered separately.

1. It is easiest if a rule is **"content neutral" as to time, place, and manner of application**. This means that the library may require borrower cards to check out materials, but only if it requires all borrowers to have cards, and imposes the same rules on everyone for getting them. A library can require proof of current address, for example, but only if it requires this proof from every applicant, not just those who look like they may be transients.

Libraries may establish rules which are not content neutral, but the rules must then meet much more stringent tests. Among other things they must meet a "compelling" (as distinct from a "significant") state interest to survive. A compelling state interest is a reason for a state law, rule, or policy which is strong enough to justify abridging a person's constitutional rights. An example would be a public safety law which limits or prevents free speech.

2. The rules must be narrowly tailored to the **purpose** of the institution, and must be designed **to protect a significant government interest**. If the purpose of the institution, and the significant government interest in it, is to collect, preserve, and make available to the people books and other information, then the rules must be related to this. A library may not adopt rules which have little or nothing to do with its basic purpose.

An example of a defensible "tailored to the purpose/significant government interest" rule would be loan periods: the library's job is to make materials available, and it can set up procedures for doing that. A rule against playing a radio so that others can hear it is also reasonable because doing so prevents others from exercising their right of access to information and ideas.

On the other hand, it is seriously questionable whether a rule about wearing shirts in the library is defensible on any but health and safety grounds (and to me, those are dubious at best). What, after all, does covering one's chest have to do with acquiring information, or the library's ability to provide it? Surely, wearing shirts is an aesthetic issue, not one which impinges on the basic purpose of the library.

Attorney Lahey also points out that libraries should make clear—by stating it over and over again—that their rules are designed to promote the significant government interest of protecting the people's access to information and ideas. This is necessary, among other reasons, to minimize losses in litigation. She suggests that a court, contemplating rules which state that a library considered the First Amendment protections when it formulated them, might view the rules more kindly.

Another reason is the opportunity the rules present for reminding people of the purpose of the public library. It is very easy, after all, for the readers of mystery fiction to forget that public libraries have a significant government purpose which goes far beyond recreational services, popular and important as those services may be.

3. The final First Amendment test is that a library rule which prevents someone or some class of people from access **must leave open some alternative channel** for receiving information and ideas. The Supreme Court ruling on the Hare Krishna case cited above explains this criterion in simple free speech terms. The ban on soliciting cash donations (although not on leafletting) inside airport terminals was upheld on the ground that the solicitors could solicit outdoors in front of the building. They had an alternative place to do it.

A library may find providing "alternative channels" rather more difficult. After all, how many other places are there in a community where a person can receive information or ideas? A rule banning patrons for "offensive" personal hygiene (body odor), for instance, has the effect of excluding groups of people who don't have access to bathing facilities. A list may be offered of community shelters which have showers, along with a promise that the person can come back to the library when he or she has used them, but that is at best a weak "alternative channel."

There is another piece of constitutional law which affects both the rules libraries make and how they are enforced: the guarantees of due process and equal protection contained in the Fourteenth Amendment to the Constitution. Although the concept has changed over the years, basically due process means (according to Daniel Oran's *Law Directory for Non-Lawyers*) "that a person should always have notice and a real chance to present his or her side in a legal dispute. . . ." The government (in this case, the states) cannot adopt laws which are arbitrary or unfair. And, the laws they adopt must provide definite standards for enforcement.

Equal protection (and due process) is what Richard Kreimer asserted he had been denied in the *Kreimer v. Morristown* case: he claimed that the behavior rules the library adopted denied him the same protection of the law enjoyed by other classes of persons. He was being treated unequally, he said, because he was homeless, and did not have access to the bathing facilities which the library's "personal hygiene" rules required. He also maintained that the Morristown library rules were vague. As noted, the Third Circuit Court of Appeals did not agree, but a lesson from the *Kreimer* case is that any library should be exceedingly careful in the way it defines its rules.

In fact, a library which expects to enforce a specified odor regulation would be wise to develop some objective critieria for making its judgments. Bruce Ennis, counsel for the Freedom to Read Foundation in the *Kreimer v. Morristown* case, has suggested possible objective tests, although he proposes them only as examples: three other patrons must complain before a "smells bad" rule is invoked, or the library director and some number of patrons must agree that another patron smells intolerably bad.[8]

The subjectivity involved here is both dangerous and demeaning. Perhaps the American Library Association should commission high tech wizards to develop a "smell-o-meter" which could standardize our judgments. That way we could decide how to score someone who smells heavily of perfume or cologne, too. Some people are allergic to these sorts of fragrances; others are merely offended by them.

The smell-o-meter could come in two models. Model A would be for libraries with really big odor problems. It would attach to the front doors, and measure everyone who walked in. Presumably bells and whistles would go off when someone flunked.

Model B would be hand-held (say the size of a barcode reader) and would be kept behind the circulation desk. When a patron complained about someone's body odor, special staff, probably dressed in white jump suits and boots, would quickly descend on the offensive person and measure him (or her), sort of like what the security guards in airports do.

I am of course joking about a very serious business because I think there are better ways to deal with smelly patrons than trying to enforce personal hygiene rules. We'll discuss the issue more in Chapter 3, which is about street people.

Local Laws and Ordinances

The great thing about local laws and ordinances, from the public library's perspective, is that there are so many of them. Over the years, our states and municipalities have managed to legislate practically everything that affects the security of a library building and its collections. This enables the library to post the law, cite the source (e.g., City of Worthy Ordinance Number 6792), and blame its putative unfairness on someone else. Look for rules about damaging property, harassing other people, and panhandling on public property in this category.

The bad thing about some local laws and ordinances is that they may not meet the First Amendment tests described in the previous section. For example, back in the 1950s many public libraries in the South had segregated reading rooms, restrooms, water fountains, and the like, mandated by local ordinance. The antigay ordinances of the 1990s may have the same effect.

It is also true that many city attorneys, county counsels, and other governmental legal advisors do not necessarily have special expertise in matters of information theory and law, free speech, or the special status of libraries as limited public forums. Their long experience in reviewing public works contracts may have left no time for thinking of the library in any terms but those of recreational reading. The librarian's task has to be to educate these legal officers if possible, and if not to find alternative legal advice. The surest source of good advice will be the American Library Association's Office of Intellectual Freedom, or your state library association.

Local Custom and Culture

Legally, the most tenuous basis for making rules and regulations governing library use is "local custom." But this is the thin ice upon which many libraries' conduct codes are based. Sheltering with the majority yields a feeling of security, not to mention political protection. And indeed, this is a very comfortable position, right up to the moment when librarians and their trustees are hauled into court by a litigious rule violator who has read the First Amendment.

In its best application, local custom helps sort out rule-making issues into two categories: those which everyone can agree on right away, and those which are going to have to be carefully negotiated.

Presumably the first category would include prohibitions against smoking, damaging library materials, or eating and drinking in the main reading room. In the second category fall all the rules and potential rules which will fail the First Amendment tests unless they are very carefully crafted indeed: the ones about loitering, or smelling bad, or sleeping, or harassing the staff.

"Local custom" may be the rubric attached by the Library Board, the City Council, the Friends, or even the staff to their own definitions of appropriate behavior, but it is astonishing how frequently (and quickly) real disagreement emerges about what local custom actually is. Fortunately, these disagreements provide the opportunity for assessment of the library's situation, and its need for rules, in terms of larger legal requirements.

Writing Rules That Work

There probably isn't a librarian alive who doubts the premise that it is better to have planned ahead than to be stuck with no procedures at a moment of crisis. When you come upon a couple in a carrel near the 900s engaged in what can only be described as explicit sex, it is surely a thousand times better to know exactly what to do, than it is to stand there with an incredulous look on your face wondering why they didn't teach you about this in library school.

Making rules and policies in advance allows one to consider the situation, whatever it is, objectively, and outside the context of the particular perpetrators of the moment. As discussed above, this is very important in the context of the First Amendment. But even if that weren't the case, it makes for better policy.

Getting ready for both the predictable and the unpredictable gives the rule-writer the opportunity to step back and think, "What is the problem here? What change in the situation would fix it? Are we facing situations in which a rule is the answer, or would staff training in how to handle varieties of behavior be a better approach?"

The problem, for example, might be that a number of library users like to bring coffee and Danish from the take-out place on the corner into the main reading room. The resulting trash is attracting pests, and more than one cup of coffee has been knocked over onto reference materials or has stained the rugs.

The obvious solution is to make a rule which says no food or drink in the library, although better phrasing might be "No Eating or Drinking," or "Eating and Drinking Are Permitted in the Lobby Only." For the purists among your patrons, with the latter language you aren't forbidding people to have candy bars in their pockets.

Ah, but you are wondering how to write a rule forbidding carrel sex, and the answer is, you shouldn't even try. This is a true story, by the way — it happened at the Central Branch of the Santa Cruz Public Library. The staff person who handled it said to the participant he could see, "I don't think that is appropriate behavior in the library, do you?"

"No," she said, "I don't," and the couple desisted. If they hadn't stopped, he would have warned them, and eventually called the police, because lewd and lascivious behavior in public places is illegal in California.

The real question here is how often a library staff is actually confronted with that kind of behavior. The answer is rarely. And therefore, a rule forbidding it, particularly a posted one, does little more than make the library look silly. Think about it:

WELCOME TO THE PEOPLE'S PUBLIC LIBRARY!
No Smoking (City of Worthy Ordinance # 6793)
Eating and Drinking Are Permitted in the Lobby Only
No Overt or Explicit Physical Sexual Behavior,
Either Alone or with a Partner

The same applies to rules forbidding firearms. If a library has a real problem created by patrons carrying guns and displaying them, would it be solved by posting a rule which proscribes

> Carrying a weapon into the library unless authorized by law. Any patron authorized to carry a weapon must notify the library staff that he/she is carrying a weapon in the library.[9]

It is very doubtful that that would remedy the situation. Would the sort of people who habitually carry guns bother to register them at the front desk? A library visited on a regular basis by gang members or others carrying weapons needs a full time police presence more than it does a posted rule, and that is the issue it should spend time addressing.

There are laws in nearly every state and local community which ban lewd behavior, carrying and displaying firearms in a manner which endangers the public, drinking alcohol or using drugs in public, and a variety of other behaviors which are inappropriate because they cause problems in a library. If a library is tormented by these kinds of behaviors on a regular basis, then the statement it ought to post is:

> The Library staff will apply all local ordinances and state laws which govern behavior in public places as well as those regarding defacement of public property, and call the Police Department to help enforce them when necessary.

It is true, however, that there are certain rules a library may wish to post, even if local or state laws apply. A ban on smoking is a good example. Although these days smoking is prohibited in many public buildings, lots of people who smoke need to be reminded of that. Razor-blading out the pages from magazines constitutes abusing public property, and is also illegal in most jurisdictions. But the library might prefer to post a rule about damaging library property just to make sure there is no confusion.

A library might also wish to consider establishing a rule limiting use of certain library areas to patrons who are actually using the materials contained in that collection. The obvious example of this is the Children's Room, where the library can use such a rule to help itself create a safer environment for children. Chapter 5 on sexually deviant behaviors discusses this matter.

There is some disagreement among librarians and their supporters as to whether a library really needs to actually *post* its rules at all. The side opposed argues that, provided a copy of the rules is available for scrutiny at a public desk, posting the rules is a negative image which only gives people bad ideas. They suggest that if a problem develops, giving a violating patron a clear oral warning, as well as a statement of the consequences of failing to comply with the rule, is all that is required.

Others believe that regardless of whether the law actually requires it, the rules we set for behavior must be posted so that there is no confusion as to what they are. One reason is that some signs, as for example those for No Smoking, are so ubiquitous that their absence authorizes the behavior. And as one librarian pointed out, "It may be true that after a while the posted rules become part of the furniture, and no one sees them, but I feel a lot more comfortable sending staff out to deal with problems if I know we did our best to inform people ahead of time of what we expect from them."

The specific rules the library decides it does need to post should be written in language which makes a clear statement of the unacceptable (or acceptable) behavior: "Please talk in soft tones only" is a better rule than "Quiet please." "Children under 9 must be supervised by a person 14 years of age or older" is a very specific statement which covers two problems at once: young children left alone at the library, and young children in the care of young siblings.

Common sense suggests that the consequences of not following the rules should also be stated clearly. Probably this is best done at the top of the posted rules:

> If you fail to follow the Library's behavior rules, the staff may require you to leave. Damaging or destroying library materials, equipment, or furniture can result in suspension of your library borrowing privileges, as well as criminal prosecution.

One problem in writing good rules is balancing the needs of the larger group (either patrons or staff) with those of individual users, especially in the context of First Amendment rights. By the same token, a library needs to protect the rights of the larger group too. No one denies, for example, that people with physical disabilities have the same rights of access to information as those without. But, for instance, does a hearing impaired user over in the Periodicals Area have the right to shout comments on the news of the day to his companion? And the companion to shout back?

It may be that the balanced approach will have to be achieved in the enforcement, rather than in the rule itself. The staff, for instance, may tolerate the hard-of-hearing person's voice level when he or she is asking for information or help, but insist on reasonable quiet when the conversation is merely social.

There is one final test to apply to all the rules the library makes. It is standing back, looking at the rule, and asking, "Is it possible to misconstrue this rule? Is there any way anyone could use this rule to discriminate against someone else?" If the answer is yes, start again. And when you do that, start by asking (again) what problem the rule is intended to solve. Is a rule a good method for mitigating the problem situation, or would better enforcement techniques by the staff help more?

Caution: any rule that has anything to do with physical appearance probably falls in this category. Even a rule which says a patron must wear a shirt and shoes offers room to quibble over the definition of shoes (are sandals shoes?), as well as what "wearing" really means, not to mention the definition of a shirt. Does "wearing" include a shirt hung over naked shoulders? Maybe in the eyes of a tired circulation desk worker, invoking the rule will depend on whether the shirtless person is tanned and clean shaven, or bearded and dirty.

With all of the above in mind, here's a check list for evaluating library behavior rules as they are conceptualized and written:

1. *Does the problem behavior interfere with anyone else's right to use the library?* If it doesn't, don't bother to make a rule about it.
2. *Is the problem behavior already covered by local ordinance or state law?* If so, is there a good reason why the library needs to restate it?
3. *Is a rule an appropriate means for substantially mitigating a situation caused by the problem behavior?* If it isn't, find another way to address the problem. These could range from special staff training to cooperative approaches with other community agencies.
4. *Does the rule address a situation created by problem behavior, or is the rule really aimed at a specific individual or a group of people?* If it is, find another way to deal with him/her/them.
5. *Does a rule forbidding this behavior meet First Amendment tests?* Is it content neutral? Is it tailored to the purpose of the library and does it protect a significant government interest? Does it leave open an alternative channel for receiving information and ideas?
6. *Can the majority of people understand the wording used to write this rule?* This is not an issue of whether the library's rules should be posted in languages other than English: of course they should be if the library has significant user groups who have English as a second language. The issue is deciding whether most of the library's patrons will understand phrases such as "failure to mitigate the loud and obnoxious behavior will result in immediate. . ."
7. *Can the majority of people understand what will happen if they don't follow the rule?*
8. *Is the rule clear enough so that there is no possibility that a member of the staff can misconstrue it?*
9. *And a year later, do we still need this rule, and does it continue to meet the first eight criteria?*

If all your rules can survive this examination, then get them printed and posted. Next up is exhibit policies and meeting rooms.

NOTES

1. *Richard R. Kreimer v. Bureau of Police for the Town of Morristown et al., Free Public Library of Morristown and Morris Township et al.*, 959 F. 2d 1242, No. 91-5501, U.S. Court of Appeals for the Third Circuit, decided March 23, 1992. Hereinafter cited as *Kreimer v. Morristown*.

2. *Kreimer v. Morristown* [p. 23].

3. *International Society for Krishna Consciousness, Inc. et al. v. Lee, Superintendent of Port Authority Police*, No. 91-155 U.S. Supreme Court [decided June 26, 1992] 92 Daily Journal D.A.R. 8871.

4. Cited in *Kreimer v. Morristown* [p.23].

5. *Kreimer v. Morristown* [p.25].

6. *Kreimer v. Morristown* [p.31].

7. Kate Lahey, Esq., "Do We Control Our Own Buildings?" Remarks presented at Public Library Association and American Library Trustee Association Program of this title, American Library Association Annual Conference, San Francisco, California, June 28, 1992. Also, telephone interview by author, August 10, 1992.

8. Bruce Ennis, Esq., "Patron Behavior and Access to Information: The Legal Issues." Speech presented at Public Library Association Hot Topics Program, American Library Association Annual Conference, San Francisco, California, June 30, 1992.

9. New Jersey Library Association. "Draft Rules for Conduct in Libraries." *New Jersey Libraries Newsletter*, June 1992, cited in *the Unabashed Librarian*, Number 84, p. 4.

2.   *Exhibits and Meeting Rooms*

If carrel sex doesn't drive you to taking a serious look at your procedures for handling problem situations, then the possibility of getting up one day and reading either of these two headlines in the morning newspaper certainly will:

NEO NAZIS TAKE OVER LIBRARY DISPLAY SPACE

or

MAN-BOY LOVE GROUP MEETS AT LIBRARY

The neo–Nazi display was at the Santa Cruz Public Library in 1990, and although it did not provoke a crisis in print, it was only because the sponsor of the exhibit did not have the media savvy to create one. He had ample grounds, because the director of libraries disobeyed fundamental strictures of the *Library Bill of Rights* by pulling the exhibit. I was that director. And it was only in the aftermath of this event, when I set out to clarify my library's policy on public use of exhibit space, that I developed an understanding of the First Amendment and other issues involved.

As for the "man-boy love" group, it put the meeting room use rules of the San Francisco Public Library up for public debate, aided and abetted by reporters for the *San Francisco Chronicle*. The SFPL staff and library commissioners had been scrupulous in their attention to the *Library Bill of Rights*, and their handling of an issue in which there was wide public interest provides interesting lessons, discussed in the second part of this chapter.

Exhibits and Display Policies

The American Library Association's Intellectual Freedom Committee gives us the most direct guidance in developing exhibit and display policies. Its recommendations were adopted by the ALA Council in 1991, and appear in Appendix B as "Exhibit Spaces and Bulletin Boards, An Interpretation of the *Library Bill of Rights.*"

The Interpretation's basic point is that if a library is going to make display space available, either for its own use or for the public, it should do so on the same basis as it selects books and other materials. Nothing should be excluded because of "the origin, background, or views" of the person or group creating the exhibit. Materials shouldn't be removed because someone doesn't agree with the point made, and exhibit space should be made available "on an equitable basis, regardless of the beliefs or affiliations of individuals or groups requesting their use." All these are points and quotations enumerated in the *Library Bill of Rights* (see Appendix A).

And all these are points which are sometimes easier to honor in the abstract than in reality. For example, the Santa Cruz Public Library System had an exhibit and display policy which worked well right up to the moment of crisis. The policy stated that exhibits could be mounted in the various display cases by any not-for-profit group or individual, on any subject of interest to some segment of the community. It included careful wording about the library system's lack of insurance for displayed materials, added after a thief broke into one of the cases and stole a handcrafted necklace. It specified that branch managers were in charge of exhibits at their facilities, and it outlined a first come, first served reservation procedure.

Exhibits ran the gamut from displays of rocks by the Santa Cruz Gem Society to informational presentations mounted by community groups advocating particular points of view (e.g., the Save Our Shores group on off-shore oil drilling). The staff rather prided itself on its broad and liberal display policy. It was careful to book pro and con exhibits: "right to life" one month, a "pro choice" group the next. Whenever controversy was anticipated, a notebook for writing comments was put out, "in order to facilitate public debate."

All of this was thoroughly in keeping with the general character of the community—educated, politically active, and reasonably tolerant of most points of view, cultures, and life styles.

In the summer of 1989 the Christic Institute mounted a display which advocated that group's program of world peace and rapprochement with the Soviet Union. An individual complained to the staff about the exhibit, and requested display space to express an opposing point of view. His material was booked for the coming March, which was the first available date.

It was installed in a case in the front lobby of the Library System's Central Branch, the same facility which had housed the Christic Institute exhibit. While some of the display was indeed information about the Soviet Union, fully 80 percent was blatantly racist and anti–Semitic: photocopies of the *Protocols of the Learned Elders of Zion*, advertisements for reports disputing the existence of the Holocaust, and a rewritten version of "Jewess Poet" Emma Lazarus's Statue of Liberty poem: "Give me your tired and useless scum, your diseased social outcasts. Your huddled masses of worthless blacks, browns, and yellows yearning to be free . . ." and so forth.

Public outrage was immediate. The reference and circulation desk staffs, as well as the branch manager and the director of libraries, were inundated with lengthy complaints, which ran along the lines of "How can we allow an exhibit of such hatred in a tolerant community like Santa Cruz?" Several staff also expressed themselves as personally humiliated that such a display could be mounted in a place they worked, and threatened action by their union if it was not pulled immediately.

The director removed the exhibit on the ground that the content did not reflect the individual's advance agreement with the library staff. The materials were returned to the sponsor, along with a letter explaining why. He subsequently complained vociferously to the director, making relatively incoherent threats of legal action, but none were ever filed.

The staff then set about the business of revising the library's exhibit policy so that this kind of display could never happen again. The director proposed wording which empowered the staff to reject exhibits which contained material which was "racist in content, or material which denigrated or insulted any race, sex, religion, ethnic group, or nationality, or any individuals or population groups identified by sexual preference, disability, or illness."

The city attorney, who reviewed all policies with legal ramifications, accompanied his absolute rejection of the draft with a copy of the Seventh Circuit Court of Appeals opinion in the case of the *National Socialist Party of America v. Village of Skokie, Illinois*.[1] And he included a rather acerbic note which implied his surprise that a librarian (of all people) would be so ignorant of the people's right to free expression.

The final policy the Library System adopted a month later may not precisely meet every requirement of the ALA *Library Bill of Rights* interpretation, but it goes a long way towards doing so. The discussion which accompanied development of a final revision proved to be educational for everyone involved. And while neither the library staff nor its overseers would relish ever having to countenance an exhibit of the neo–Nazi type, they would do so because they now understand why they must.

It is a matter, again, of the First Amendment to the U.S. Constitution, which guarantees the people's right to free speech. As a public library, and a limited public forum for expressive rights, if we make exhibit spaces available to the public, we must do it on an equitable basis. We may adopt "time, place, and manner" rules for use, but only if they are "content neutral" and applied equally to everyone. They may not be applied "on the basis of the doctrinal, religious, or political beliefs of potential users."[2]

However, nothing in the *Library Bill of Rights*, or the Exhibit Interpretation, says that each individual exhibit must contain balance, any more than every book must portray all sides of an issue. The balance requirement applies to the library's overall program or calendar of exhibits.

Libraries do not have to make their exhibit spaces available to any "outside" person or group if they regard the whole business as too much hassle. Instead, they can limit displays to those created by their own staffs, although these too must present a balanced viewpoint.

On the other hand, exhibits — on the walls, on bulletin boards, or in display cases — are a very useful tool for promoting the library mission of meeting the information needs of the people. Since the library is obligated to present "a broad spectrum of opinion and a variety of viewpoints," exhibits can be used to facilitate public debate on topics of current local and national interest, in ways which the mere presence of books or videos cannot.

The Exhibit Interpretation of the *Library Bill of Rights* encourages libraries to adopt a written display and exhibit policy if they do make space available to outsiders. The policy should use *inclusive*, rather than exclusive, language. In other words, it is better to say what kinds of groups *may* sponsor exhibits (e.g., educational, cultural, intellectual, or charitable), than to lay down a blanket rule against displays by religious groups (which might meet the intellectual criteria), or all commercial enterprises (isn't a ceramicist who sells her work in business?).

The most effective written policies always start with a statement of what the purpose of the policy is. This is also a helpful means for educating the library board and the public about the function of exhibits in the library's program.

A well-written exhibit policy will then go on to outline the other rules for use, being careful to distinguish between the rules for bulletin boards and display cases, if there is a difference. Time, place, and manner rules should be specified, including size criteria if appropriate. The reservation procedure, and the rules for set-up and take-down should be included. It is always a good idea to insist that the sponsoring individual or group identify themselves in the exhibit. If the library cannot insure the exhibit contents it should make this clear.

One useful means for ensuring that exhibitors understand the rules is to incorporate them into a reservation form, which also lists the name, address, and phone number of the exhibitor, specifies the contents of the display and the appropriate dates, and has a "release of liability" statement which the exhibitor signs. Make sure both the library and the exhibitor have copies.

Finally, library boards and staffs may wish to make clear to the public that they do not agree with or support every item displayed in the facility or housed in the collection. The ALA Exhibit Interpretation suggests that libraries "may wish to post a permanent notice near the exhibit area stating that the library does not advocate or endorse the viewpoints of exhibits or exhibitors." At the Santa Cruz Library System, we now have this message posted on every display case and bulletin board.

The foregoing comments relate to the most common type of displays found in public libraries: the ones on bulletin boards, in cases, or on display panels. But some libraries have what amounts to art gallery space at their disposal, and the policies for allowing the public to use it require special thought.

Is the library board, or the staff, or users, going to be pleased to see nudity, "obscenity," lurid depictions of violence, political commentary, and other common but controversial subjects of art, hanging in the main lobby or in the upstairs hall, "Where," as an indignant citizen might put it, "we can't help but look at it"?

Community display space for local artists is nearly always at a premium, and thus opportunities for shows at the public library will undoubtedly be very popular. But given the First Amendment constraints placed on libraries, it is not possible for the library to exert anything except "time, place and manner" controls over art exhibits.

If a library decides it wants to go ahead with gallery-type art exhibits anyway, there are at least two things it ought to consider. The first is location. If in fact the gallery space is on a main route, which no one, adult or child, coming in and going out of the library can avoid, think again about whether having art exhibits is so valuable to the library's information program that board and staff are willing to handle whatever public outcry arises. If the proposed display space is reasonably separate, there probably isn't anything to worry about.

The second issue is who decides what gets exhibited. One option is to establish a jury, composed of outsiders, such as arts teachers, to choose artists to exhibit. Another is to ask the local arts council to take over management of the whole business: selection, installation, publicity, and so on. In either case, the outsiders can give the library art shows the imprimatur of official expertise, while at the same time relieving the library staff of arguments with the public or local artists ("We have a Jury which chooses which shows will be mounted. The Chair's name is . . ."). Of course in its charge to its art jury, the library staff needs to make clear that only "artistic" criteria may be used in evaluating work for display.

One final issue should be addressed in a display policy about works of art: sales by the artist. The only law involved here is local. A library can allow an artist to put prices on the work, and display her or his business card, or avoid the taint of commercialism by limiting information to display of the card only. Let local preference be your guide.

The Exhibit Policy of the Prince Georges County Memorial Library in Hyattsville, Maryland, appears in Appendix E as an example.

Library Meeting Rooms

The First Amendment to the Constitution not only guarantees the basic liberty of free speech, it also guarantees the right of the people to freely assemble to speak. Of course, the right of free assembly is not worth much if the people have no place to meet. This happens to be a right that many people want to exercise — a fact well known by the staff of any public library with a meeting room. Most such rooms are booked so heavily by community organizations, that the staff often needs to get its own reservations for library programs onto the schedule long before it actually knows what the content of its program will be.

Heavy public demand for meeting room space, particularly the kind of comfortable, accessible-to-the-disabled, and usually inexpensive space a library offers, is the strongest reason why a public library needs a clear written policy governing meeting room use.

The American Library Association's Intellectual Freedom Committee makes recommendations for this policy: "Meeting Rooms: An Interpretation of the *Library Bill of Rights*" appears in Appendix C. The same basic strictures which govern exhibit and materials selection policies apply to meeting rooms: the rules must ensure equity of use, regardless of the beliefs or affiliations of the sponsors.

For many years public libraries (and the American Library Association) worked under the assumption that they could, if they wished, bar religious and partisan political groups from using their meeting rooms, presumably on "separation of church and state" grounds, and the desire of any publicly funded agency to maintain strict political neutrality. They simply had to do it equitably — all religious groups denied, all partisan political groups denied, etc.

However, in the late 1980s a religious organization called Concerned Women for America brought suit against the Oxford (Mississippi) Branch of the First Regional Library for denying it the right to use its auditorium for a Prayer Chapter meeting. The library lost at the federal district court level, and on appeal at the Fifth Circuit Court.[3]

The library's meeting room policy at the time of the court case reads a lot like what we'd probably find in a great many public libraries across the country:

> The Auditorium of the Oxford Branch of the First Regional Library is open for use of groups or organizations of a civic, cultural or educational character, but not for social gatherings, entertaining, dramatic productions, money-raising, or commercial purposes. It is also not available for meetings for social, political, partisan, or religious purposes, or when in the judgement of the Director or Branch Librarian any disorder is likely to occur.[4]

The library staff testified that in practice, having established that the group was meeting for neither religious nor political purposes, and that the calendar date was available, it would book the auditorium for practically any group. Past uses included a local child's piano recital, a closed meeting of U.S. Navy recruiters to discuss recruitment strategies, and a meeting of the Oxford Swim Club.

The Court ruled that by opening up its meeting room to diverse groups which were not directly linked to the library's mission, the library had created a public forum for First Amendment expressive rights. As a public forum it could not deny use by any group on the basis of the content of the group's speech or viewpoint. Thus it could not exclude religious or any other groups.

A meeting room may be a public forum, but it is secondary to the primary and fundamental purpose of the library. Therefore, the library can prevent uses which disrupt or undermine its basic purpose. How far a library needs to take this option in formulating its policies depends in large measure on the dimensions of the problems it confronts.

One of the most interesting recent examples of a conflict of this nature occurred in San Francisco in 1991.[5] A reporter for the *San Francisco Chronicle* "uncovered" the fact that an organization called the North American Man Boy Love Association (NAMBLA) had for years been meeting at one of SFPL's branches. Accompanied by tremendous public outcry, pressure was placed on the Library Commissioners to adopt regulations for meeting room use which specifically forbade use of library facilities to NAMBLA and to all groups who advocated comparably unpopular views.

The reality was, however, that NAMBLA's by-laws (which had been submitted with their original meeting room use application) were a carefully constructed statement of the organization's advocacy for the abolition of "age of consent" laws, and absolutely eschewed actions which promoted unlawful conduct. In other words, NAMBLA's meetings were a classic exercise of the First Amendment right to free speech, peaceful assembly, and to petition the government for the redress of grievances. And therefore, they could not be denied the right to use a San Francisco Public Library meeting room.

The Library Commissioners did decide to revise the library's existing meeting room use rules, however, since they had been in place for some years. This caused them to clarify their definition of the role public meeting rooms play in the program of the library. They agreed that the meeting rooms were limited public fora because they are secondary to the primary and fundamental purpose of the library, which is "to provide a safe haven for study and contemplation,"[6] and in particular, to provide a place where parents can send their children without concern for their safety.

Since the library can prevent uses which disrupt or undermine its basic purpose, it could adopt rules for meeting room use which do this. Crucial, though, is the emphasis on uses of meeting room space. It is not specific groups which can undermine the library's basic purpose, but rather the use they make of the facility.

Among other policy revisions, the San Francisco Library Commissioners decided that all its meeting rooms could and should be considered part of the same system, with the staff the arbiters of where a particular group should meet. This would make it possible for the director to decide, for example, that a group which attracts people who could be considered dangerous to children, or would discourage parents' confidence in the library as a safe haven for their kids, could be assigned to space away from those branches with large constituencies of children.

The North American Man Boy Love Association disappeared from the library when the Commissioners also decided to adopt a rule which specified that all meetings must be open to the public, and posted that rule in each room.

Nothing except local desire and local needs requires libraries to make their meeting rooms available to "non-library" organizations; use may be limited to library-related activities only, "provided that the limitation is clearly circumscribed and is viewpoint neutral."[7]

If the library does decide to let outsiders use its meeting room, it may make rules for use which protect the library's basic purpose and mission. These include place, time, and manner restrictions, including frequency. The most useful meeting room policies will also cover several other points.

Many libraries require that any meeting held on library premises be open to the public. This may be mandated by state and local law, and, as San Francisco believes, it can be useful in making the space less attractive to potentially controversial groups (if that is what the library wants to do). Another reason for the rule is that it helps limit use to community groups needing more than committee sized space. If meeting room space is at a premium in a community, the library may not want to "waste" what it has on groups of six or seven people, who will have an easier time finding a smaller space. Libraries can offer either "must be open" or "may be closed" options, provided the same standards are applied to all groups.

Another important question is whether the library will allow user groups to charge admission to events. There are three issues here. The first is covered by ALA's Meeting Room Interpretation: Article V of the *Library Bill of Rights* states that people should not be denied use of a library on the basis of their origin, age, background, or views. "It is inconsistent with Article V," reads the Interpretation, "to restrict indirectly access to library meeting rooms based on an individual's or group's ability to pay for that access."

Another issue is the library's potential share of the "take." Many groups want to charge admission to their event in order to raise funds for their own programs. One reason they are using the library meeting room, instead of renting commercial space, is to take advantage of the inexpensive public facility, thereby maximizing their profits. Many librarians would argue that if the group is raising money by using a publicly subsidized facility, the "owner" of the facility should get a fair percentage of the proceeds. This may be difficult to work out, and a real hassle to administer, but the library should consider the issue carefully as it develops a meeting room policy.

Finally, on the matter of charging fees for admissions, libraries should check carefully about local admissions tax law. If a group charges admission and is required to collect such a tax, the library would be wise to provide an information sheet about procedures to any group booking its meeting room space. Even if the library is not liable for enforcing the admissions tax law, this is a worthy service it can provide to a community group which may have only the vaguest idea what its local tax obligations are.

Just as with exhibit policies, it is a very good idea to ensure that meeting room users know and understand the library's rules. A reservation form listing the rules, which can be copied after it has been filled out and given to the group, saves no end of trouble later in an argument over whether the sponsors did in fact know that they were responsible for "returning the room to the condition in which they found it," or some comparable local rule. An example of a Meeting Room Policy (Santa Cruz's) appears in Appendix E.

Here's another check list to use in reviewing your exhibit space and meeting room policies, or creating new ones. Again, the usual disclaimer applies: rely on your own attorney for legal advice.

1. Are exhibits mounted by nonlibrary groups, and meeting room use by the public, a part of the library's overall program of service? If they aren't, don't bother.

2. Do the rules for exhibits and displays, and for meeting room use, meet the First Amendment tests? Do they relate only to time, place, and manner, and can they be applied equally to everyone, no matter what their beliefs?
3. Is the overall program of exhibits, whether sponsored by the library or by "outsiders," balanced in its presentation of points of view?
4. Are the meeting room rules focused on the use to which the room is being put, rather than on who is sponsoring the meeting?
5. Are the rules for mounting exhibits and displays, or using the meeting room, written and published in such a way that everyone, even the least experienced user, can understand them?

NOTES

1. *Frank Collin and the National Socialist Party of America v. Village of Skokie et al.* Nos. 78-1391, 78-1385. United States Court of Appeals, Seventh Circuit, 5/22/78.

2. "Exhibit Spaces and Bulletin Boards. An Interpretation of the *Library Bill of Rights.*" Adopted July 2, 1991, by the American Library Association Council.

3. *Concerned Women for America v. Lafayette County and Oxford Public Library.* No. 88-1743. United States Court of Appeals, Fifth Circuit, September 14, 1989.

4. Ibid.

5. Material about the North American Man Boy Love Association and the San Francisco Public Library is based upon two sources: American Library Association, Public Library Association and American Library Trustee Association, "Do We Control Our Own Buildings?" Program at Annual Conference, June 28, 1992 (Cassette Tape ALA-231), Remarks of Burke Delventhal, deputy city attorney, and author's interview with Delventhal, August 21, 1992.

7. "Meeting Rooms. An Interpretation of the *Library Bill of Rights.*" Adopted July 2, 1992, by the American Library Association Council.

Part II

Problems That Plague Us

3. Street People, the Mentally Disabled, Substance Abusers, and Other Symbols of Our Times

Let's face it. The boring majority of library problems are caused by everyday patrons who are angry and take it out on the library staff. Indeed, these often take consummate skill and patience to defuse. But they seem so normal: the "glamour" problems of the 1990s — situations involving street people, mentally disabled people, substance abusers, and the like — are what most library workers want to know how to handle. So let's start with these, and come back to angry people in Chapter 4.

There are two issues here. The first is how library staff should handle the specific problem situations that street people — including the mentally disabled and substance abusers — create. Never mind, for the moment, about potential limitations on their right to be in the library, and what the larger community response to the problem should be. The reality is, they *are* in the library, and their behavior can create problems for staff and for other users. How should we handle that?

The second issue is how public libraries should cope with the fact that as poverty and other social ills increase in this country, the number of people on the streets with nowhere else to go (and therefore hanging around libraries) is also increasing. Are public libraries being turned into dumping grounds for society's problems? If they are, what can we do about it?

First, some definitions. "Street people" is the term I am going to use in discussing the raunchy looking folks, usually men but women too, who tend to travel with most of their worldly possessions in trash

31

bags or bedrolls, wear very ragged clothes, often haven't bathed lately, and may or may not exhibit various eccentric or antisocial behaviors indicative of mental illness, alcoholism, or other substance abuse. The defining characteristic of the street person in this chapter is *appearance.*

In other times street people were called "vagrants," a term which has legal weight, but is no longer much in fashion. "Bum," "beggar," and "hobo" have also been used. In some river towns street people are called "trolls" because they often camp under bridges. "Transient" comes closest in some ways to describing the population that worries library staffs and users, but that description still is not sufficient.

"Homeless people" are not necessarily street people, which is why I am not using that more common term. In fact, the majority of homeless persons in the nation are single mothers and their dependent children. And these days there also are plenty of neatly dressed men and women with jobs who have no place to live. They are not the ones who are causing problems for public libraries. Nor are all alcoholics or mentally disabled persons street people. We all know about alcoholics who apparently lead normal lives, and people with serious mental illness who are not living on the street (but some of whom come in and create library problems anyway).

What problems a street person causes depend on what rules for behavior a library has adopted. A street person is not a problem simply because of his or her appearance or putative life style. It is what the street person does in the library which may or may not create, a problem for the library staff.

A "mentally disabled" person is defined here as someone who, regardless of appearance, acts out in a dysfunctional way, creating a disturbance which breaks a rule or otherwise interferes with someone else's right to use the library. For example, a Midwestern public library has a patron we'll call Mrs. Wallace. She is a neatly dressed woman in her late forties who likes to read mysteries. A frequent library visitor, she conducts conversations across the library table with her companion, whom we'll call Mrs. Righter, often in a loud voice.

The problem is that Mrs. Righter does not exist, except of course in the mind of Mrs. Wallace. Mrs. Wallace is mentally disabled. We'll come back to this situation to learn how a clever library staff member solved the problem this nonthreatening but disruptive person was creating.

A "substance abuser" is anyone who is wigged out on alcohol, drugs, or whatever, and is causing a problem for other library users because of it. Lots of people abuse substances without preventing someone else from using the library: eating too much or smoking heavily comes immediately to mind. I am emphasizing this simple-minded point only to remind us that we are focussing on problem behaviors here, not generic categories of people.

Coping Techniques and a Lengthy Example

Since the *Kreimer v. Morristown* case, I've heard many library workers, when discussing problem situations with street people or the mentally ill, say "I didn't want to violate his rights. I was afraid if I did the wrong thing I'd get the library in trouble—that he'd sue us or something."

We need to get to the common ground. We don't want to violate users' rights. We don't want them to violate our rights or the rights of other users. It is the responsibility of library management to ensure that the library has rules for behavior which meet constitutional requirements, and that staff is trained to enforce them equitably and sensibly. If management has done its job, no library worker should have to worry that she or he is violating someone's rights.

I suggest four tools to help a library staff cope with the problems created by street people, mentally disabled people, and substance abusers in libraries. The first three can be taught with staff training: knowing the library's rules and how to enforce them, remembering to consult one's colleagues, and using teamwork to deal with specific problems.

The fourth tool is common sense, an attribute which rarely appears in a job description, but is crucial for most library workers. It may be a genetic trait, but common sense definitely can be improved via experience and training.

Here's the lengthy example. I use it because it illustrates the worst of all possible scenarios: a tiny branch potentially overwhelmed by the problems created by one mentally disabled person.

The Santa Cruz City County Library System was recently host to a mentally ill, quasi–street person patron (he was an off-again, on-again resident of halfway houses) I'll call Gene. Gene had visited several branches, everywhere creating problems, ranging from obnoxious body odor, through shouting, to sexual harassment of staff. His choice of branch location depended on where he was living at the moment.

Gene was physically imposing: six foot four, 230 pounds, beard, dreadlocks, and a big, deep voice. His behaviors seemed to be motivated by desire for attention. He talked loudly to himself and imaginary people, making repetitive statements such as "I am a powerful Black man." He mumbled and grunted. Periodically he asked help at the reference desk in finding materials, but his requests were repetitive. He remembered certain people, such as a branch manager, but he did not have any long term memory for rules or consequences. For this reason, it did not do any good to ban him from the library for three days as a "lesson" or punishment, because on the fourth day he'd be back with the same behavior.

Accosting women was one of Gene's typical behaviors, especially if the woman was African American. He also sometimes tried to touch young children, particularly African American children and those who were on their own, although this did not seem to be sexual behavior so much as simply finding human contact.

Gene's modus operandi was to come into the branch and establish himself in a reference area chair for the day. There would be no particular problem with this, except that his recent branch of choice was very small (only one large room). Since Gene rarely bathed or changed his clothes, his sometimes nauseating body odor dominated the branch. He also wanted to be in physical contact with the branch's page (an African American college student). He'd follow her about from book stack to book stack, trying to stand close to her.

And Gene was a shouter. Asked to leave, or to go outside for awhile, he would stand on the entrance steps and complain about life in general and the status of Black men in society. None of his comments made much sense, but his stage-like presence by the door did have a chilling effect on people visiting this small town branch.

Barbara Kiehl, our branch manager, hit easily on one of the tools needed for handling this kind of situation: "The other branch managers clued me in," she says. "He isn't dangerous, but you do have to be completely straightforward. If I wanted Gene to be quieter I had to say so, and tell him what would happen if he wasn't. In the first days, I guess I let myself be intimidated by him, and spent too much time just putting up with him."

Barbara also told me that after she noticed Gene looking over the younger children at the branch, she took the branch's three frequent latchkey girls aside and encouraged them to be sure to tell her if anyone they didn't know tried to touch them. A few days later one of the children indeed reported that Gene had tried to sit too close to her, and that she had told him to go away. Barbara immediately told Gene to cease and desist, and warned him she would call the sheriff if he touched a child again. He stopped that behavior.

The problem with the page required implementing the advice we have received from trainers who are expert in teaching women to defend themselves: make the unacceptable behavior clear to the person doing it, set limits, and stick to them. The page had to steel herself to say to Gene, "No, I do not want you to stand there. You are standing too close to me. You are preventing me from doing my work. Please stop it."

This clear statement enabled her supervisor to deal directly with violations of the limits set, escalating eventually to a call to law enforcement if this was necessary.

When Gene smelled so bad that in the opinion of the branch manager he was interfering with other people's right to use the library, she asked him to leave. She told him he could come back when he had washed himself and his clothes. She knew he had the means to do this, because at the time he was living in a nearby group home. And yes, this was a judgment call.

Did she use some version of the smell-o-meter? No, even California doesn't have that technology yet. Did she get three patrons to agree? No, the Santa Cruz Library System hasn't made a behavior rule which requires complaints from a specified number of other patrons in a small branch before the branch manager can politely ask a person to leave (see Chapter 1). We rely on the common sense and judgment of the branch manager who is on the site. One reason is that we know what smells bad at a branch the size of Barbara's wouldn't be noticed at the much larger downtown facility.

We expect the branch manager to evaluate the situation. Has anyone complained? Are people moving away from the area where he is? Are you yourself made sick by the odor? If any of these apply, ask another staff person to smell the area. If you both think the odor is interfering with other people's rights, tell the offender to leave until he has cleaned himself and his clothes.

Gene's talking and shouting behavior on the front steps of the library presented a special problem because it occurred outside the library, potentially locating him in the territory of a traditional public forum. On the other hand, nobody is allowed to block the entrance of a public building, and the entrance steps are narrow. With a more litigious-minded person, this might not have worked, but Barbara solved it by telling him, "This behavior is inappropriate. If you don't stop right now and move on, I will call the sheriff." And in court the library would certainly have argued that Gene was stopping other people from using the branch.

Barbara also reported that she called the group home where Gene lived to talk with the supervisor about persuading him to bathe more frequently. She didn't get very far: "No, I can't do anything about that" and "No there is nothing I can do" was the unhelpful response. We'll return to this supervisor in the second part of this chapter.

In the meantime, the story of Gene and the small branch ended with the news that he was required to move out of his group home, and stopped coming to that library. So this particular mentally disabled–street person problem for our small branch evaporated when Gene moved away (although he was spotted at the downtown branch a few weeks later, meaning that the library probably hasn't seen the last of Gene and the problems he creates). But suppose that coincidental solution hadn't happened? What would the branch manager have done next? It seems to me there were two options.

The first was to continue to endure, taking the same decisive approach: when Gene's talk was too loud, telling him he had to be quiet or to leave. If his body odor was too great, telling him to go and clean up—the library worker's directive in this case apparently carrying more weight than that of the group home supervisor. If he touched a child or harassed a page, the same applied, with escalation to law enforcement if necessary.

The alternative in dealing with a situation like this is to create a case file which can be used to secure a court order preventing the person from coming into the library. As director of libraries I would have had no objection to doing this in Gene's case. He was abusing a tiny branch by seriously interfering with its intended purpose as a public library and with the rights of other people to use its resources. The judgment might well be different at a larger facility, where staff and patrons have many more options for seating and so forth.

Getting a court order against a patron is a strategy which needs the cooperation of the library's legal counsel and local law enforcement officials. Meeting with them before there is a case in hand, and agreeing on how this strategy might work, are absolutely crucial. They will tell the library staff what documentation is needed, and it is up to the library to create staff procedures which ensure that the data is there when push comes to shove.

The usual case file includes a complete log by the branch manager of every encounter with the patron, what both the staff and the patron did or said, and what the outcome was. Verification by other staff (the page, the library clerk) would be required. Also needed, but hardest to obtain, would be supporting statements by other patrons.

It is a sad comment on our times that people are willing to complain about problem situations, but are so frequently unwilling to take personal and "official" responsibility for what they don't like. A staff person says, "I'm writing down what you say. Will you sign it please, so that we can use it if we have to call the police?" And the patron says, "Oh, no. I can't get involved in anything like that." This is the same person who thinks "they"—meaning us—should do something about such-and-such a problem.

My own conviction is that a direct statement to a complaining patron is the best strategy. If someone objects to someone else's behavior, and then says she or he won't put her name on the dotted line, tell her/him that the library cannot find permanent solutions to bad behavior by an habitual offender if other patrons aren't willing to make official complaints. At least try to extract the patron's name and phone number for the file, so that if the library does end up requesting a court order, he or she can be tracked down for a statement.

And I hope no one has missed the obvious point that good record keeping is crucial. Any library should have a standard form on which the staff can report incidents of one sort or another. Ongoing situations, such as the ones created by Gene, should be logged by the branch manager, who may end up finding that keeping a Gene Diary (or whatever) is satisfyingly therapeutic.

Handling Gene involved knowing the library rules and how to enforce them, consultation with other library staff, and a strong dose of the branch manager's common sense. I want to add a few more words on the latter trait.

Part of common sense, it seems to me, is accepting people, even mentally disabled people, for who and what they are, and dealing with them on their own terms. One of my favorite examples of this is a story told by Julia Orozco, the director of the Salinas Public Library in California. A patron was banging, banging, banging on the key-board of one of the public access catalog terminals. A staff person asked him to stop, and he said, "I can't. I'm telecommunicating with the spirits."

The staff person looked at him and said, "This is the wrong terminal for that," and she managed to ease him out the door.

Further east, in the Memphis–Shelby County Library System, one of the branches had a patron who liked to copy pieces of fruit on the copy machine. Every couple of weeks he'd come in and spend time making photocopies of real sliced oranges or grapefruit. Naturally enough, the staff was not particularly pleased by this behavior, al-though the library doesn't have a posted rule saying "No Copying of Fruit." The copier glass had to be cleaned every time he came in, so one day a staff person approached him and said, "Mr. Jameson, I understand that you need to copy fruit. We need you to clean up the copy machine afterwards."

"Oh," said Mr. Jameson. "Okay."

And the next time he came in, he copied fruit as usual, and then took a paper out of his pocket and wiped down the copy machine. End of problem.

Remember Mrs. Wallace, who talked too loudly to her imaginary friend, Mrs. Righter? Once, when a staff person approached Mrs. Wallace and asked her to lower her voice, she said, "I can't. Mrs. Righter keeps asking me questions and she's hard of hearing, you know."

"Oh," said the staff person. "All right. Mrs. Righter, will you please be quiet now?" And Mrs. Righter was, and so was Mrs. Wallace for the rest of that day.

Teamwork in handling problem situations is crucial, and the term means more than simply two people approaching a scary patron, or one staff person backing up another in a difficult encounter. It is also collectively developing responses to difficult situations by consulting and comparing notes.

A year of so ago the Santa Cruz Library System had a nine year old kid who specialized in being super-demanding. He was very bright and seductively curious, but there was no satisfying him. He wouldn't let go once a staff person started helping him. Robert, we'll call him, would ask question after question, obsessing on a subject. And he'd repeat and repeat the same question, moving from one public desk to another, insisting on far more help than any individual can reasonably demand in a very busy library. He'd come back, too, the next day, with the same question, or another, and start again.

Staff conversation established that the child who had become a problem at all desks at Central and at his neighborhood branch was, indeed, the same Robert. The collective, creative response was to devise a ticket system for the child that would limit his access to staff help.

The staff didn't feel right about limiting service to a child without explaining to the parent, so they phoned Robert's mother. Surprise! She told them that Robert is a "high functioning autistic" child, versus the hyperactive diagnosis we had made. Coming to the library is part of his entry into the world, his mother said. He is learning how to handle real world situations, which is why she comes in with him, but only sits and reads magazines, and doesn't intervene in his interactions with the staff. (We all knew we signed on as psychotherapists, right?)

The real world experience we devised for Robert was to make tickets for him in the Children's Room at the Central Branch. His neighborhood branch manager does the same thing. Each ticket entitles him to one question on one subject. When a ticket is used up, the staff person involved says, "I've helped you all that I can." He watches while the staff person puts a big check on the slip, and then throws it away, physically emphasizing that the question is done. When he has used up all his tickets for the day, the staff person says, "I've helped you all that I can. Now you need to find something else to do." The precise language in each case is part of the programmed response.

I am aware that anyone reading this story who works in a big city library will believe that only a small town operation could afford to put this kind of attention into finding a "fix" for the problems created by one small patron. I'm not so sure that's true, for the simple reason that Robert was driving everyone crazy. It was easier for the staff to get together and figure something out, than to leave the solution to chance. Wouldn't that be true in a big library too?

One thing about the Robert case which aggravates me, however, is the expectations of Robert's mother. The library staff are neither social workers nor special education teachers. She nevertheless assumed that because we were there and available, we'd be able provide the "real world" experiences her son needs. She had no thought for how difficult our staff might find the child's tormenting behavior, nor that the staff had obligations to other patrons which might be sacrificed to meet Robert's needs.

The tempering factor in creative responses of this sort is available staff time and energy. I can imagine situations in which Robert might have to be limited to one question per day, for instance. But it is hoped that the instinctive response—"Get this kid out of my hair"—will not be allowed to overwhelm the prudent operational compassion which should be a hallmark of library dealings with the mentally afflicted.

Appendix F, the Santa Cruz problem situation manual, also contains interleaved sample procedures from other libraries for handling street people, mentally disabled people, and substance abusers. These samples have one particularly important common theme not yet mentioned: if a staff person has any reason to believe that a patron—especially a substance abuser—is dangerous, call the police. If you are at a geographically isolated facility, get backup from someone else—the sheriff, the fire department, someone—before you approach the patron.

Symbols of Our Times

In his fascinating 1992 book, *The Visible Poor—Homelessness in the United States*,[1] Joel Blau makes the point that people get angry with street people and beggars (the "homeless" in common parlance) because it is very hard to avoid actually seeing them. Other kinds of poverty endemic in our society—single mothers on welfare, migrant farmworkers living in camps with no toilets, elderly people alone in single room occupancy hotels—can all be avoided by the simple means of organizing one's life correctly. It is much harder to miss the sight of a "derelict" sitting on the Main Street sidewalk, or a street person reading the newspaper at the public library.

The first response of far too many people to the sight of poverty is anger at the victim. And when the victims use the community institutions, such as libraries, which people regard as their own (even if they don't want to spend a lot of tax money supporting them), they get even madder. They generalize and stereotype, labeling anyone who fails to meet their standards of dress and hygiene as a "street person homeless bum." They transfer anger to the library staff for "putting up with those people." And they dramatize their lack of comfort with the unknown by expressing fears for their personal safety.

The irony of the situation, of course, is that many of these same complaining people are not willing to address the systemic economic and social problems which have created the "visible poor" in the first place. This leaves public libraries and their staffs in the wretched position of needing to honor the First Amendment rights of everyone to use their facilities, at the same time that their traditional support constituencies back out the door in disgust at who is also using the library.

I don't have a solution to this problem, but I do think libraries can take a two pronged approach to finding one. The first involves education of their traditional users and supporters, and the second is community organization for change.

Standing up for the First Amendment right of all people to have access to the information the library provides is an obligation of all public library workers, both because it is the law, and because it is right.

First we must adopt behavior rules which ensure that no one interferes with anyone else's right to use the library. And we must train our staffs in how to enforce those rules equitably. Then we must be willing to say to our library board members, donors, regular mystery readers, politicians, and anyone else who asks, "We do not make aesthetic judgments about who can use the library. *You* have to tell *me* how that person whose looks or smell you don't like is interfering with your library use." It is not easy, but if you say it often enough, people eventually begin to understand.

The public library staff is also entitled to say to its community, its governing authorities, and its newspapers, "Wait a minute. We are the public library, and we have a very difficult and complex job to do meeting the information needs of all the people. You must confront, whether you like it or not, the fact that there are a lot of poor people in this community who have nowhere to go all day. They come to the library, which is their right, but providing day center service is not our job. What can we do about this?"

That is basically what Pat Woodrum, director of the Tulsa (Oklahoma) Public Library, did some years ago, when a large population of homeless people was occupying the library's main facility. After one false start, she managed to get the Community Service Council, churches, members of the Library Commission, and other groups to work together to find a solution to the problem — a day center at which the library has a deposit collection and other services are provided.[2] And the solution has held. In late 1992 Woodrum reports that the center is now constructing a new, larger building, with added services.[3] Meanwhile the Tulsa library continues to provide the day center with a depository collection, issuing borrower cards to people who use the center's address, and operating a literacy program for the homeless.

Woodrum used persistence, and her library's long tradition of cooperation with other community groups to deal with this problem. I also suspect that she was ultimately successful because she was willing to be direct in her statement of the need, to say to the people of Tulsa, "We have a problem here. What are *we* going to do about it."

Remember the Santa Cruz branch manager who got the run-around from the group home supervisor, when she called to see if he could do something to get Gene to bathe more frequently? In retrospect, I am sorry we didn't call the county mental health department, and raise a tremendous stink about that response. The group home was operating under a profit making contract from the county. The supervisor's job was to care for the people who lived in his facility, and he should have been grateful that a worker from another agency was trying to reach out to help one of his clients. Instead he dismissed us, because he thought he could get away with it. We should have demanded action, and if we didn't get it, should have reported him to his funding authorities.

It is important to remember that there is a difference between being "abrasive," which heaven knows no librarian wants to be, and being willing to say out loud and directly what the problem is. My conviction is that librarians need to improve their skills in this. We need to say loudly that we are in the information business, not the shelter business, and that if shelter is the need, the community is going to have to find a way to meet it. We will help, but we will not do the whole job.

Ten Minutes a Week for Training

Every library does its best to train new workers in standard policies and procedures, usually after going through a hiring process which attempts to weed out the people whose communication skills are not strong enough to make it on the public desks. And most libraries try to send staff to occasional training workshops on special subjects.

However, what with budget crises, and automation system upgrades, and constantly increasing demands for services, it is very easy for even the best of libraries to fall down in its program of ongoing training.

Avoid this if you possibly can; training and retraining for all staff is immensely important. It helps them stay fresh, it reminds workers of what library policy is, and it provides therapy for people who are working in relatively stressful situations.

Another important reason why a library should find a way to make sure that ongoing training gets done is the window it provides supervisors on what is really going on in any library operation. Staff talk when they get together, and they tend to talk turkey if they are sharing information about problems. Listening to them is a great way to pick up on trouble situations before they get out of control.

One idea for institutionalizing a library's ongoing training program is to allocate ten or fifteen minutes out of every staff meeting for some sort of problem situation exercise. These can be the meetings each library department holds (the monthly meeting of the youth services staff, the biweekly circulation staff meeting, and so on) or the whole staff meeting at a branch. The point is to spend a little time, frequently, practicing and discussing how the staff handles problem situations. If you make role-playing assignments (when appropriate) and do the training exercise at the beginning of the meeting, you'll cut down on late arrivals (no one likes to miss the entertainment) and make sure you actually get the training done.

Here are four discussion questions related to handling problem situations created by mentally disabled people, substance abusers, and street people. There are no right answers—how a staff should respond to each problem depends upon the library's own procedures.

1. A page trying to shelve books runs her book truck into a backpack which has been left in the aisle. Just as she is moving it out of the way, a man who smells like a brewery comes up and says, "Listen, bitch, don't you touch my stuff." What should the page do?
2. A patron comes to the desk to complain about a dirty-looking person sitting in the reading room. How does the staff person respond?
3. The director has had a call from the chair of the library board, who wants to know whether the library gives borrower cards to homeless people. The chair thinks the board ought to adopt a policy on that, and wonders what the staff would recommend.
4. A teacher turns up one morning with a group of eight obviously mentally retarded adults. The teacher doesn't ask for special help from the library staff, but other patrons are clearly very disturbed by the group. One of them finally complains. What should the staff do or say?

NOTES

1. Blau, Joel. *The Visible Poor—Homelessness in the United States.* New York: Oxford University Press, 1992.

2. Woodrum, Pat. "A Haven for the Homeless." *Library Journal*, V. 113, January 1988, pp. 55–57.

3. Woodrum, Pat. Interview, November 16, 1992, by telephone.

4. *Dealing with Angry People*

At a recent training session for library workers in Southern California, the first half hour was spent on a warm-up exercise which turned out to be fun for everyone. The group was asked to list the problems they had with library users which drove them the craziest. Probably about 60 percent of the workshop participants were circulation desk clerks and other public service support staff, so they really knew what goes on in libraries. Drunk and disorderly patrons, smelly street people, latchkey children, and sexual deviants were all mentioned.

But the overwhelming majority of the problems cited were those created by people who are angry at the library: mad because of an overdue notice they think was an error, mad because an item requested two days ago still isn't in, mad because they had trouble finding a parking space, mad because they couldn't find the deeply desired book on the shelves, mad because the library is closing at 9 p.m., mad because . . . You name it, a patron has gotten mad about it.

Judith Drescher, the director of the Memphis–Shelby County (Tennessee) Public Library and Information Center, suggests that the reason people get mad at the library is because their expectations are so high. They don't expect much from the Post Office or the Department of Motor Vehicles or even a department store. They expect to have to stand in line forever at government agencies, and to obey rules such as needing your credit card if you want to charge something.

But libraries are supposed to be different. They are pleasant places, with comfortable chairs, and they have books and magazines, and even videos and records. And the staff, who are often one's friends, or the daughter of one's neighbor, are nice too. They smile, and help you find things.

So when the library enforces a rule, such as needing your card to check something out, or dares to send you a notice about a book you know you returned last week, or fails to get you something you really want to read right now, *WELL!!* It is unexpected, unreasonable, wrong, and well worth getting mad about. What is the world coming to, after all, when even the library starts sending those awful computer printed notices one can hardly read, and can't even keep bestsellers on the shelves? And so forth.

This chapter is about helping staff deal with people who are mad. "Active listening," coupled with reasonable assertiveness and a few tricks collected from libraries around the country, are the basis of the coping techniques described.

There is a lot of literature on personal communication skills, some of it written specifically for libraries. Anne Mathews' *Communicate!* and *The Assertive Librarian* by Janette S. Caputo are two examples of the latter, as are various articles in library periodical literature.[1] There are also quite a few psychologists, social workers, and academics who run sidelines in communications training, so it shouldn't be hard to find an expert to do a staff workshop if your library (or better, your library consortium) can afford it.

Basically, I want to make two points. The first is that every staff person at every level, from book shelvers to the director, needs to have good communications skills to handle the problems they'll confront in the library world. For those on the service desks, these skills include knowing how to keep cool and keep smiling when an angry patron is making every effort to provoke the opposite response.

The second is that sometimes even patrons are right: if an anger-making situation keeps coming up, probably the staff should take a look at the problem causing it, rather than worrying about whether or not the angry people are wrong to be mad.

Communications Skills

I once heard a police officer who specializes in community relations say that he is astounded at how little time the typical police academy puts into training cops to communicate well. "We don't just hand them a gun and say 'point it and fire it' do we? No, we put them through days, even weeks of firing practice, and they have to requalify every year. But we don't do anything like that with communications skills, and they use those more than they do their guns, or they ought to, anyway." He saw effective communication skills, and the need for training to acquire them, as one of the similarities between cops and library workers. The essence of effective communication, he thought, was translating what people said into what they really meant.

This is also a part of "active listening," the technique Thomas Gordon popularized by turning it into Parent Effectiveness Training. The active listening idea is to acknowledge (or accept) the other person's feelings, so that the two of you can get on with finding out what the real problem is. It also uses the "I-messages" and "You-messages" of assertiveness to establish ownership of ideas and emotions, and defuse tense situations.

Here's an example of active listening from an article Nathan M. Smith and Irene Adams wrote for the periodical *Public Libraries*:

USER: Boy, what a crummy library! Who organized this place anyway? This is the biggest mess I've ever seen!

STAFF: (Using nonactive listening) Yes, it could be better organized, but that's only one opinion. We do our best to make it work. If you really have a complaint, take it to the director's office.

The trouble with this response, Smith and Adams point out, is that it is defensive, and doesn't recognize that the patron is simply taking his frustration out on the librarian. A better, active listening response, would be:

STAFF: It sounds like you've had a frustrating experience. Is there any way I can help you find what you need?[2]

Frankly, I've always been faintly embarrassed by active listening examples. Reading them on the page, I usually feel about as comfortable with them as I did telling my adolescent son, "It makes me feel very annoyed when you don't clean your room." What, after all, could be more asinine than saying to a person with steam coming out of her ears, "You seem to be very upset." That kind of remark feels to me like an invitation for a punch in the nose, as in, "You bet I am, cookie, and you better just watch it."

However, I must confess that active listening has gotten many a teenager's room cleaned up, and often works to defuse the ire of people in unreasonable moods. The major problem is remembering to use it. It could be that this is harder for library directors than it is for desk staff, who, after all, get much more day-to-day practice handling difficult people. In either case, practice helps, so be sure to read the last part of this chapter which gives some advice about training sessions.

Since active listening is a "first step in the process" technique, what comes after it is important too. Communications specialists suggest that only 10 percent of everything we say is content. Another 30 percent is body language (eye contact, relaxed posture, etc.), and the balance is the tone of voice. To demonstrate the latter, try saying this sentence aloud putting the emphasis on a different word each time:

> **I** didn't say you stole the book.
> I **didn't** say you stole the book.
> I didn't **say** you stole the book.
> I didn't say **you** stole the book.
> I didn't say you **stole** the book.
> I didn't say you stole the **book**.

What we are after in good communication is a perfect match between what we are saying, how we say it, and what our body is demonstrating we feel.

The Paraphrasing Technique

One technique that incorporates the principles of active listening and works well in getting through an angry encounter, is to paraphrase what the patron is saying, and try to make the patron paraphrase you right back. Here's an example of how it works. The scene involves a new patron, who has been asked to give his driver's license number as identification.

PATRON: But that's totally stupid! Why do I need a driver's license to get a library card? I just want to check out a video, not drive through the library.

STAFF: What I hear you saying is: "I don't see why I need a driver's license just to get a library card." Is that what you're saying?

PATRON: Yes. Why should I have a driver's license to use the library?

STAFF: We need to see a driver's license because the DMV is the only way we have of tracking down people who move and take the library's books with them. If you don't have a driver's license, a DMV ID is okay. Have I made the reason clear?

PATRON: I guess so. You are going to use people's license numbers to find
           them if they steal books.
STAFF: Right.

When people are very upset, they tend not to listen to each other. Instead, they spend the time the other person is talking thinking up what they will say next. Paraphrasing forces both people to listen, so that they can restate the other's position. Thus it is especially useful when the conflict is very emotional. Paraphrasing does, of course, require a "contract" between the partners, and that is not always easy to achieve.

At a minimum, though, a staff person can repeat back what the patron has said, and make slow progress towards getting the library's point across.

The "I Believe You" Technique

This technique is used by the staff at the Memphis–Shelby County Library to handle patrons who claim that they already have returned an item for which they have received an overdue notice.

PATRON: I got this notice, and it really makes me so annoyed. I know I
           returned this book, and this is the second notice I've gotten for it.
STAFF: I believe you. Tell you what . . . Here's what we can do. Give me
           your card, and let's get your record up on the screen. (Wands in
           borrower card, turns circulation terminal so that patron can see the
           record too.)
              Now, here's the item listed as overdue. I am going to mark it
           "Claims Returned," because that is what the computer calls it when
           we show the item as still out, but you say you returned it.
              We'll look for the item here and at the other branches, and I hope
           you'll look around at home too. Have you tried under the front seat
           of the car? I'm not joking—if we had a dollar for every time some-
           one finds a book there, the library would have a much bigger
           budget . . . Okay?
PATRON: Well, is the book going to stay on my record forever?
STAFF: Not if we can find it. Or maybe you'll find it. Why don't you check
           back in a few weeks and see if it has turned up.

The Memphis policy is to clear most patron records, although it does keep track of how many "claims returned" items a patron has reported over the years. But whether patrons are forgiven for items which never turn up is not the point. What's important here is the basic positive style of the staff response to the patron.

The Stand and Deliver Technique

Sometimes a patron is too angry for active listening, or paraphrasing, or even "I Believe You" to work. The patron is furious, and wants a chance to express his or her rage to someone from the library. No staff person needs to listen to abusive or obscene language from a library user, but sometimes this kind of anger can be defused by using the "Stand and Deliver Technique." It is called this because the staff person stands there and the patron delivers anger.

The staff person listens attentively to what the patron says, nodding appropriately, and working hard to stay calm and not appear combative. Staff makes no attempt to respond in any way, except perhaps for occasional murmured affirmative sounds such as "uh huh" and "hmmmm." There is no point in trying to interject information or ask questions, because the patron would simply interrupt.

Eventually, the patron will run out of steam. Then the staff person can begin, calmly, to state the library's position on the problem. But it is important here to avoid arguing with the patron. Better is for the staff person to restate the library's position over and over again—like a broken record.

And if it is finally clear that there is no way the staff person is going to be able to get the patron to let go, the matter should be referred up the line to a supervisor or to the director. Suggest that the patron write a letter to the director, or telephone: sometimes angry people feel better when they can talk to the "the boss." Anyway, management gets paid more, so why shouldn't they have to handle difficult people too?

One library director points out that the worst problem with angry and verbally abusive patrons is the psychological damage they do to staff. It can take an hour or more for a staff person to recover emotionally from a "stand and deliver" encounter, unless she has learned and incorporated into her consciousness the old Zen lesson: when an insult spear is thrown at you, move your head. One reason for identifying a "handling" technique, and giving it a memorable name, is to help staff objectify the situation—to move their heads instead of getting emotionally speared.

A Few More Tricks for Promoting Civility at the Front Desk

Periodically we all need to remind ourselves that while it is true that patrons can behave very badly, there are also certain behaviors by public desk workers which cause patron annoyance, and should consequently be avoided by staff at all costs:

- Embarrassing an adult in front of his or her children.
- Embarrassing a teenager in front of his or her peers (especially his, but girls don't respond well to this treatment either).
- Cold or marginally hostile demeanor, or simply failure ever to smile.
- Inability to make eye contact with the person being served.
- Continuing conversations with colleagues while waiting on a patron.
- Calling users by their first names when not personally acquainted.
- Talking in jargon, e.g., OCLC, LC, periodical, PAC, interface, ISBN, monograph, serial, and so on.
- Calling anyone younger "honey" or "dear."
- Making users feel even sillier than they already do for asking a question.

Looking at the Situation Which Causes Problems

The Memphis–Shelby County staff used the "I Believe You" technique to solve a problem they were having with video collection users. The library charges $1.50 to borrow a video for three days, and lots of patrons used to bring them back with complaints (the staff thinks that was simply because actual cash money was involved): the video wasn't rewound, it didn't work on the patron's VCR, it wasn't the movie the patron thought it was going to be, and so forth. They wanted their money back. But giving a refund for each $1.50, or crediting the borrower's account, was far too complicated to be a serious option.

The circulation desk staff thought up this solution. Whenever a patron returning a video complains, the staff person says, "I believe you," and offers the patron a coupon for one free video checkout. No questions, no arguments.

So lesson one is that well prepared staff can defuse anger, and get what's wanted even from hostile transactions, if they are clever about it and use the right language.

But lesson two is equally important: a library staff has to be flexible in its approaches to problems. And management has to be willing to evaluate rules, policies, and procedures in terms of real life at the public service desks. Which is more important: maintaining the good-will of a lot of library users, or extracting $1.50 for every video borrowed? If a well-meant rule or procedure, even a seemingly neces-sary rule or procedure, is generating a lot of surplus complaints, considering alternatives may be in order—the more creative, the better.

And there is a lesson three in this example: another reason why it is important to cast a fresh eye on "problems" is because sometimes it turns out that they are more apparent than real. This is especially true with ones involving angry patrons, since everyone remembers a loud complaint from a user longer than a grateful smile. The Memphis–Shelby County Library had 10,000 coupons printed up when this "I Believe You" strategy was implemented. Over the next ten months the staff distributed an average of 58 coupons per month, which comes out to 2.5 coupons per library branch at a cost of $3.75 per branch. It was a problem which disappeared.

Psychologist Perry Buffington has noted that forward-looking corporations in the United States have begun to take complaints from customers a lot more seriously than they used to[3] (and yes, just as in a science fiction movie, you may have to suspend disbelief to accept this assertion as any kind of blanket proposition. But the basic point is sound). The traditional approach was to put the newest, least experi-enced worker on the complaint phone, and give the customer lip service.

These days, however, says Buffington, businesses are looking at complaints as an opportunity to gain information about their products, and as a chance to consolidate their relationship with customers. Even if the complainer isn't completely satisfied, he or she feels better about the company if a real investigation is made.

Training staff in problem solving, e.g., thinking up creative solu-tions to problems we didn't know we had, is part of this process for corporations. And it might also be useful for libraries too. But the most important point here is that while we all know that library users can on occasion be *very* unpleasant, it is nevertheless wise to pay attention to what is making them mad.

There will certainly be things about which the staff can do nothing (at least for the time being). Adding more parking spaces in a crowded downtown is one example. But has the number of "claims returned" complaints been rising recently, as in "I *know* I returned this book just two days ago, honestly!" Wouldn't it be worth at least discussing taking a look at the notice-sending sequence to see if it could or should be lengthened?

Front desk and other staff should be asked to log complaints (an appropriate code system can help make this possible), even the ones they settle happily, just to make sure there aren't things which are falling through the cracks. And if library management is truly interested in finding answers for making library life easier for everyone, the front line staff should also be actively involved in the search for problem solutions.

Ten Minutes a Week for Training

Here are some active listening scenarios, developed for the aforementioned Southern California workshop, which might be used in a staff meeting at which the training topic is handling angry patrons. They envision pairs of staff, one playing the angry patron, and the other the active listener.

> Library user has come to the library several times looking for a book, without success. He now complains, "What's the point of a library if the books I want are never available?"
> User objects strenuously to paying an overdue fine, and claims angrily that she *did* turn in the book on time—it must be the staff's fault for not getting to the returned item. Or maybe it got lost in the library. Or something!
> User objects to the library offering books in Spanish and having bilingual English/Spanish signage. English is America's language—why do librarians go out of their way to encourage those people not to learn English?
> User complains that the library is really noisy and she doesn't like coming in when it's this way. Why don't the librarians do something about it.[4]

Of course, active listening isn't always an appropriate response. There's the anecdote—which I hope is fanciful—about the library worker who first practiced this newly learned technique when an anguished patron rushed up to the circulation desk, asking "Where's the men's room."

"It sounds like you really need the men's room," responded the clerk, giving him a direct and sympathetic gaze and then maintaining a slow, careful demeanor as she fetched him the key.

The balance of the tale involves some mess on the way to the restroom — an outcome which surely added to the day's list of angry user complaints — not to mention some resentment from the custodian crew.

NOTES

1. Caputo, Janette S. *The Assertive Librarian*. Phoenix, Ariz.: Oryx Press, 1984.

Mathews, Anne J. *Communicate! A Librarian's Guide to Interpersonal Relations*. Chicago: American Library Association, 1983.

2. Smith, Nathan M., and Irene Adams. "Using Active Listening to Deal with Patron Problems." *Public Libraries*, July/August 1991, p. 236.

3. Buffington, Perry W. "Capitalizing on Complaints." *Sky*, June 1991, pp. 33–38.

4. These scenarios were developed for a Santiago (California) Library System Training Workshop, "Patron Problems, Librarian Solutions: Dealing with Difficult People," September 16–17, 1992, at Orange County Library Headquarters, Santa Ana, Calif.

5. *The Nasty Behaviors: Sexual Deviancy and Parental Child Abuse*

Reports of libidinous outbreaks in supposedly staid libraries tend to draw nudges and snickers. Haven't we all—in library school or starting on the job—heard legends about sex in the stacks? Topless readers? Fervent smooching at the homework tables?

But those are activities which, even if embarrassing and angering, are relatively easy to handle so long as they are consensual.

Far worse are the aberrant acts of deranged adults that truly interfere with the rights of others—particularly women and children—to use the library. Parental child abuse is discussed further on in this chapter. First, let's deal with the deviant sexual behaviors which are harrowingly, often criminally inflicted on library patrons and staff.

Interviews with librarians across the country produced a collection of stories—some shocking and some funny—representing an incredible range of experiences. Flashing, peeping, lurking, propositioning and touching—it is all there, a nasty intrusion in almost every librarian's working life.

One of the biggest problems with sexually aberrant behavior is that library workers can become inured to it. A college-aged book shelver may think exhibitionism is so harmless that it isn't worth reporting. And a reference desk worker may feel so embarrassed, or so tired, or so harassed by life in general, that she sees it as "coming with the territory" and too much trouble to fix.

Wrong, wrong, wrong. Part of the training of staff must be learning that *any* kind of sexual harassment is inappropriate behavior in a library, and must be stopped. The book shelver needs to understand that what she may regard as boring could frighten an older

patron or a child. And the desk worker should know that she is entitled
to better from her work situation than sexual harassment from patrons.

As librarians we have virtually no powers to enforce those laws
which exist against deviant sexual behavior. Our emphasis therefore
must be on *preventing* incidents if we can, dealing with them swiftly
when they do occur, and doing whatever we can to help the victims.
The focus of this chapter is how we can most effectively deal with the
sexual misbehavior of patrons.

First, Some Definitions

The *Diagnostic and Statistical Manual of Mental Disorders* (*DSM-
III-R*)[1] describes four paraphilias (deviations in sexual behavior) which
most of us working in public libraries will recognize. Descriptions of
each behavior are presented here because one finds this specificity so
rarely in library literature. We are all librarians, and of course we can
"look it up" if we really need to, but how often do we bother? In fact,
though, knowing at least a little about the behavior pathology can give
us confidence in dealing with the kinds of problems created for our
staffs and our patrons.

Exhibitionism is probably the most common paraphilistic behavior in libraries. An exhibitionist has recurrent, intense, sexual urges to
expose his genitals to a stranger. The person may also masturbate while
exposing himself. The disorder is apparently confined exclusively to
men.

Most crucially, from the library's perspective, an exhibitionist (or
"flasher") is not likely to be physically dangerous; his intent is to
surprise or shock his victim, and he may fantasize that the victim will
be sexually excited. But once such a person has acted on his urges,
typically there will be no further sexual activity. Exhibitionists may
expose themselves to children, but "the act is not a prelude to further
sexual activity with the child." [2] It is possible, of course, to hypothesize
a case in which an exhibitionist has multiple derangements and acts
out physically as well. But decades of police experience point the other
way, and law enforcement agencies routinely advise their staffs that
exhibitionists are nonviolent.

Exhibitionism is frequently summed up as an act designed to draw
attention to the exhibitionist. This provides some clues as to how to
handle it. For example, there is a frequently told story (surely apocry-

phal, but amusing anyway) about a stereotypical female librarian of a certain age who was confronted by an exhibitionist at the reference desk.

"Oh, you poor man!" she said to him sympathetically, shaking her head. He zipped up, left the library, and never returned again.

Knowing the exhibitionist is almost surely not dangerous is reassuring information the staff can provide to a patron who reports an incident. It also means that in almost all cases a library staff person need not fear approaching a perpetrator and taking his picture, or asking him to wait in the staff area for the police to arrive. Depending on the situation, these may not be appropriate steps to take, but if taken, in all likelihood the staff person will encounter no personal peril.

Frotteurism or Touching is rubbing or fondling behavior by a paraphile on an unsuspecting, nonconsenting person. Usually, this behavior occurs in crowded places, where the person can escape unobserved. But it can and does happen in libraries — in a line at the circulation desk, in a group around the copy machines, and so forth.

The frotteurist picks a victim whom he finds physically attractive, and who may be wearing tight fitting clothes. He rubs his genitals against the victim's thighs and buttocks, or fondles her with his hands. "The victim may not initially protest the frottage," *DSM-III-R* reports, "because she cannot imagine that such a provocative sexual act would be committed in such a public place."[3]

One obvious problem with apprehending and prosecuting a frotteurist is that characteristic behavior is to escape quickly after touching the victim.

Pedophilia, probably the most frightening sexually deviant behavior in a library setting, is defined as recurrent, intense, sexual urges and fantasies involving prepubescent children (usually those 13 or younger).

> People with Pedophilia generally report an attraction to children of a particular age range, which may be as specific as within a range of only one or two years. Those attracted to girls usually prefer eight-to-ten-year-olds, whereas those attracted to boys usually prefer slightly older children. Attraction to girls is apparently twice as common as attraction to boys. Many people with Pedophilia are sexually aroused by both young boys and young girls.[4]

Again, pedophiles are almost always men. Some are attracted to children and to adults, and some only to children. Many pedophiles were sexually abused as children themselves.

Not all pedophiles are child molesters. The definition includes sexual urges and fantasies, that do not necessarily lead to action. And not all child molesters are pedophiles; sometimes people abuse children because of other mental derangement, or simply out of desire to hurt the child's loved ones.[5]

Libraries unfortunately are prime target zones for pedophiles: men following young girls around, or soliciting boys in the bathrooms or elsewhere. One special problem is the failure of many child victims to report the solicitation or the harassment — out of embarrassment or failure to recognize it. This puts a special burden on staff to maintain alertness.

A **voyeurist** is what in slang we call a "Peeping Tom." A person with this disorder is sexually aroused by observing unsuspecting people who are naked, or getting undressed, or engaged in sexual activities. Usually the people are strangers. A voyeur doesn't seek actual sexual contact with the person observed, but might later fantasize about a sexual experience with the observed person.

Voyeurism is not the same as getting pleasure from watching pornographic films. The voyeurist's sexual arousal is based on secretive, illegal peeping. Actors in pornographic films or live performances know they are being observed.

In libraries we run into a relatively mild type of voyeurism: men standing underneath an open stair case staring up the skirts of women, or lying on the floor in the stacks, theoretically reading, but actually waiting for an unsuspecting female to come by. Like exhibitionists, voyeurs are not typically dangerous. But they certainly are unpleasant, and they certainly interfere with the right of women and girls to use the library.

Stalking and Staring is not defined by *DSM-III-R* as a paraphilia, but it is a deviancy which is apparently increasing in our society. The most famous cases have involved celebrities, but the vast majority of victims are ordinary people, including library workers. There isn't a well defined profile of the "typical" stalker, but they do seem to share some characteristics: intense interest in the media, inability to develop meaningful relationships, a history of unsuccessful efforts to establish personal identity, and a strong desire for recognition and attention. Stalkers (and starers, who might escalate to stalking) are dangerous.

Library workers who have been victimized by staring or stalking seem to have suffered most when their supervisors failed to acknowledge the problem, and did not involve the police in stopping it. One reference librarian, for example, was tormented for months by a man who followed her from place to place in the library. She was given some sympathy, but no support or help in stopping his behavior, and only when he began to follow her to the parking lot each evening were the police finally called.

This is absurd. No individual, mentally ill or not, has the right to interfere with a woman's right to do her job. Victims of this kind of harassment need to know that they should not feel guilty for resenting deviant behavior, and taking action to stop it. Library managers must take responsibility for training staff in how to cope with such behavior, and for involving law enforcement agencies quickly when confrontation doesn't work.

DSM-III-R categorizes all the other sexual deviancies we encounter in libraries as "Paraphilia Not Otherwise Specified," such as telephone scatologia, which is how psychiatrists talk about obscene phone calls. Practically anything else, from persistent requests for information about nude beaches to masturbating while reading a newspaper, can be put into one of the behavior categories listed above.

Creating a Safe Library Environment

There are several things a library staff can do to create an environment which is less likely to provide opportunities for sexual harassment of patrons. One is to implement as many as possible of the suggestions made in Chapter 8 about safe buildings: insist on good sight lines for staff in any new building, ensure that the restroom entrances are not hidden behind stacks or down dark hallways, and make the restrooms lockable so that staff can control the number of users.

Another is to ensure that all staff are trained to be alert to potential problems ("*Why* is that guy lying on the floor to read?") and to adopt a straightforward attitude toward enforcing the library's rules. A page who sees someone lying on the floor, for example, should be prepared to say, immediately, "I'm sorry, sir, but lying on the floor to read causes a hazard for other patrons. Will you please move to a chair?" It shouldn't be necessary to call in a supervisor before acting, although resistance by the patron or fear on the part of the page obviously would justify this step.

Working with the Police

Establishing a working relationship with local law enforcement officials is particularly well advised in dealing with sexual harassment incidents. It is astonishing how much the police know about what is going on (and who is doing it), and how helpful they can be if the library staff reaches out for assistance.

Reaching out is a means for jumping the real gap that often exists between library staff values (information for everyone, confidentiality above all) and those of the police (our job is to enforce the law, no one knows as much as we do about how horrible people really are). Police officers invited to consult with library staff—to lend their expertise to finding ways to handle problems—develop new understandings of how the library works, why it does what it does, and why its staff seems to be so tolerant of all those "weirdos" who use it. Once achieved at the command level, this is an understanding which will eventually be passed down the ranks within the police force, and will be an enormous help to the staff in the long run.

Among other things, the police can help lay the groundwork for getting permanent restraining or trespass orders against habitual offenders, sexual or otherwise. Another option, again requiring police understanding of the library situation, is to make staying out of the library a condition of probation. The latter usually takes less legal paperwork.

Most important, a police department which knows the staff at the library also knows that the staff will not call unless there is a real emergency or a problem of high priority.

Ensuring the Safety of Children

Providing a safe environment for children involves special problems. A library cannot (and surely doesn't want to) make a blanket rule which forbids adults unaccompanied by children from visiting the Children's Room. Staff also cannot approach people and ask them to leave, based upon their dress or other aspects of their physical appearance. Presence in the Children's Room can be limited to those who are using the children's collection, but this is not a rule all libraries care to make.

What the staff can do is keep their eyes open for suspicious behavior, such as a patron gazing steadily at a child who is clearly not a relation. The staff member should find a way to interfere. For example, the staff person can approach the starer and say, "Is there something in this collection I can help you find?" Linda Luke of the Alachua County Library in Gainesville, Florida, calls this the "Killing them with kindness" approach.

"We don't have a rule forbidding people to use the children's room," she says. "But if we spot someone who is acting like he is after kids, we try to drive him crazy with helpfulness: Can I help you with that computer? Are you sure there isn't something I can find for you? And so forth. It usually works."

Constant vigilance seems to be one key to providing a safe environment for children. Another is ensuring that the staff has its priorities straight. On the one hand, staff should not be so nervous and suspicious that they move on any adult male who dares to show his face in the Children's Room. Ninety-nine percent of all adult and teenaged men are not child molesters or voyeurs. On the other hand, when in doubt, the staff should act on behalf of children, and worry about the rights of adults later.

Boys are the targets of pedophiles as well as girls. But from an early age girls are trained and warned far more frequently about danger from "strangers." There was, for example, the wonderful child in Eugene, Oregon, who was sent off alone to the bathroom by her parent ("Why do parents *do* that?" asks the library director) and ran into a man who exposed himself to her. "The bathroom is over there," she said matter-of-factly, pointing to its door. Boys unfortunately tend to lack the radar girls develop for sensing inappropriate sexual approaches—and often, as a consequence, have less panache in handling them.

A Picture Is Worth...

Polaroid cameras, loaded with film and ready for immediate use, are a handy tool to have in any library's emergency kit. You never know, after all, when an earthquake or hurricane will hit and you will have to document the twisted shelving and books on the floor for the Federal Emergency Management Agency when there isn't a drug store open for miles. Polaroid cameras can also be used to back up staff documentation of criminal behavior, particularly sexual harassment.

When an exhibitionist is reported or observed, a member of the staff can immediately spot the perpetrator, and take his picture. The result can be used for identification purposes, to help the police, or simply as an aid for staff on the lookout for someone who is known to prey on children.

Using photography can help a library strengthen its reputation as a place where sexual harassment of staff and patrons is *not* tolerated, but it is also a tool which should be used with caution. It is legal to take photographs without the consent of the subject when there are reasonable grounds to believe that the subject is engaged or was engaged in criminal behavior. "Reasonable grounds" would be a patron or staff person reporting the incident. Taking the picture may frighten the perpetrator into a hasty exit from the library, but at least the staff then has something to give the police.

It is also very important for the library staff not to fall into the practice of taking pictures of anyone who "looks suspicious," or behaves in an unusual way.

Women who wore trousers were once viewed as very suspicious indeed. Access to the information public libraries provide is a basic right of all the people, protected by the First Amendment to the Constitution of the United States. Photography is only appropriate when criminal behavior is being investigated.

Handling Sexual Harassment Situations: Standard Procedures

The cornerstone of any staff response to a report of an incident of sexual harassment in the library must be meeting the needs of the victim. Although it is important to call the police as soon as possible, staff should be trained to give their highest priority to the victim, and let law enforcement worry about catching the perpetrator.

Appendix F offers an example from the Santa Cruz library staff problem situation manual for handling sex incidents. Its advice is pretty standard:

1. Drop everything to pay attention to the victim.
2. Treat the victim with compassion and sympathy.
3. Extract as much information as possible about the incident from the victim.
4. Armed with a description, try to identify the perpetrator. Take a Polaroid picture of him if you can.
5. Call the police and get the victim to file a formal complaint.

When a child reports being sexually harassed by someone, or "bothered" by an adult, most manuals advise following the same procedures as those for an adult, modified by the age of the victim, and the presence or absence of the child's parent.

Note: Many states require that all cases of sexual harassment and sexual abuse involving children be reported by the public official who observes them. Library management should verify whether library workers are included in the definition of "public official" under their own state's law, and the library's procedures should include instructions for staff telling how to do it (that is, how to report the incident to the police).

Harassment Not Otherwise Specified

Obscene Phone Calls

On television, when the beautiful heroine is being harassed, the script often has the phone ring, the actress answer it, listen, say "Who is this? Who *is* this?," register fear and horror (beautifully), and hang up. She is almost always wearing something you or I would save for a State Dinner at the White House.

But wearing evening clothes and whimpering into the receiver aren't how one is supposed to handle an obscene phone call. The best advice, from law enforcement officers, the psychologists, social workers, and teachers who do self-protection and assertiveness training, and everyone else, is to *hang up.* Don't give the person the satisfaction of getting you to listen. Don't do anything. Just hang up.

A library might want its staff to file reports on or log obscene phone calls, in case there is a sudden surge of them, and the police decide to investigate for a pattern. But otherwise, the basic way to handle them is to ignore them.

Stalking or Staring

The coping techniques are direct. First, the staff person should document what is happening. If, for example, she notices a patron staring at her for the second day in a row, she should write it down, noting the previous day's incident, and try moving to another work station if she can. Her object is to create a paper record which can be used with the police and courts if necessary. Of course she should report the staring to her supervisor, who should verify the facts with her or his own investigation.

Second, the staff person (assisted by her supervisor or colleague) should confront the patron and make clear that his behavior is inappropriate and unacceptable. She should say something like, "When you stare at me, you are harassing me and making it hard for me to do my work. You must stop it. Please move to another place to sit. If you don't move, you will have to leave the library." Make it clear that if the patron does not cease and desist, the police will be called. If the patron doesn't, telephone for law enforcement help. Try to photograph the patron while you are waiting.

As the understanding of stalking in the law enforcement and mental health communities has increased (along with media coverage and public awareness), we have all become more conscious of the right of women to be protected from sexual predators of all sorts. But the police cannot act if they do not know about the problem. Library managers should not hesitate to insist on decisive action, including arrest, securing court orders to forbid library use, or continuing protection for the staff person being victimized.

Other Harassing Approaches to the Staff

In Santa Cruz, California, an example of this kind of behavior was a repetitive question from the same patron about the location of nude beaches. In Gainesville, Florida, it was a patron sitting opposite the Reference Desk, making lewd gestures at, and leering and ogling, the librarian working there. He later escalated to verbal obscenities.

As with stalking and staring, the first way to cope with this kind of harassing behavior visited on staff is direct action. The staff person involved, or someone she calls, should tell the patron that he is interfering with the staff person's ability to do her or his job, and must stop immediately. If he won't, the staff will call the police. If he doesn't stop, make the call.

Handling Child Abuse in Libraries

Physical abuse of children, witnessed by staff, and what the staff is supposed to do about it, are phases one and two of a problem situation fraught with difficulties. Issues of local and state law, personal staff feelings of moral outrage, obligation and responsibility, and library confidentiality are all involved. Although child abuse incidents in libraries are seldom sexual in nature, handling them is discussed in this chapter because the typical personal response of the staff—extreme distaste and anger—is much the same as it is to sexual harassment.

Here is a story told by Librarian Meredith Pierce, who works in the children's department of the Alachua County Library in Gainesville, Florida.[6]

Meredith was staffing alone one Saturday afternoon when a woman came in with two children. It was pretty clear that the woman and the little girl, who looked to be three or four years old, were not getting along.

The mother sat the child down in a chair and told her not to move. The child wriggled. The woman snapped her fingers at her several times, and pointed in the direction of the bathroom. The child walked slowly to the bathroom, "her lip sticking out a mile and head hanging," with the woman following.

Meredith felt there was something basically wrong, so after a moment she too followed. As she arrived at the bathroom door, "I heard her striking, I heard the sound of somebody being hit real hard a lot, like maybe eight times, and you know I rushed into the bathroom. There was another child in the bathroom, and it was just a very tense, horrible situation. And I didn't know to what extent I would be allowed to intervene. So by that time she had stopped hitting the child. She was snarling at the child."

Meredith was physically reluctant to get between the woman and the child, but was relieved that at least the mother had stopped hitting. When the woman finally noticed her, Meredith said, "We have a policy of no hitting—no hitting anybody in the library." The woman said, "I am her Mother and I will thank you to stay out of this, thank you."

"She was very snippy," says Meredith. "But she stopped—my

being there stopped her. . . . She left the restroom. . . . The child was crushed and sobbing. . . I didn't want to do anything to get the library in legal trouble, but I didn't want her to be harming the child."

Meredith didn't have anyone to ask for help at that moment. Later, the woman became all "snuggle bunnies" with her child, "patting her and chin-chucking her and her little kid was just like in a coma. . . crushed and not responding." They left the library, finally, and since they didn't check out any books, Meredith wasn't able to get the name and address. "I had nothing to report," she says.

Meredith later discussed the incident with her manager, who felt that she did not have any choice but to handle the matter as she did. Her presence was enough, they agreed. She didn't need to do more because she stopped the behavior, and she couldn't do more without interfering in parental control of the child.

Meredith was reassured by this analysis, but remains haunted by the incident to this day. "Parental control of their children is a very fine line. We don't have security cameras in the restroom. I think that's why she took the child in there. And I'm still not quite clear. . . if we are allowed to come between parents and the child they're blatantly abusing."

Other librarians report physical abuse incidents which don't even occur in the privacy of the bathroom. "Adults—I assume they are parents—sometimes act as though we are furniture," comments one children's room worker. "They do amazing things, like pull a child's arm behind his back, as though we aren't even there. At my library our first strategy is to get them to notice us."

The consensus of opinion among children's librarians supports how Meredith handled the incident in Gainesville. The advice is to intervene, but in a way which objectifies the situation, using language which is not prejudicial or loaded.

Never say "Don't you hit that child. We don't allow child abuse in the library." Instead, say, "We don't allow that behavior in the library," or "We don't allow hitting in the library."

The two-fold point is to get the adult to stop, while not making the physical hostility worse. Also, you don't want the parent to come back at the child later, when you aren't there, with blame that she or he "created a problem for us when we were at the library."

Meredith wonders if there is a hard and fast rule for what action to take, and the answer, apparently, is no, there isn't. Even the legal issues are clouded. For example, as noted earlier in this chapter, many states require that public officials report suspected cases of child abuse. But such legislation is not always helpful. The California law, for example, focusses on teachers and day care workers, apparently on the theory that they are the ones who see the same children repetitively, and so are in a good position to spot abuse.

The status of librarians and library workers as "public officials" is very unclear. Can a librarian be prosecuted for failing to report abuse, as a teacher can? Which has priority: reporting suspected abuse, or maintaining patron confidentiality, which is also the law? No one has been willing to give statewide answers to these questions, so procedure is up to local preference.

All libraries should check local and state statutes, and request interpretations from their legal counsel if necessary, to find out the legal obligations of staff. And they should do it before a case of suspected abuse comes up.

Here are two other pieces of advice. Encourage the children's room staff (and all the staff if it turns out to be appropriate) to log incidents of observed child abuse, even if they are not being reported to child protective authorities or the police. This creates a paper record, which can be used in staff training and may be helpful if a legal case needs to be built later. It also helps a staff person recover from the shock and anger of the incident.

Second, children's room and other staff benefit from talking to each other about cases they have observed and how they handle them. A library might find it helpful to ask social workers from a child protective services agency to brief the staff on abuse incidents and frequency in the county, local procedures for handling, and the like.

Physical abuse of children is a problem about which we, as a society, are gaining increasing awareness. Psychologists and other health professionals, in concert with child protective workers, are struggling to find ways to stop what apparently is a growing problem in many communities. Public library staffs can participate in this process by doing what they do most effectively: ensuring that the library's collections include the best and most current information on the topic, and making sure the public at large knows the library has the information.

The best way to do those two things is to work with the professionals who are leading the community's anti–child abuse efforts. They may not have thought of the public library as a place where child abuse happens, or the dilemmas staff confront in handling what they observe.

Also, it may not have occurred to them that the public library is a place visited by thousands of adults and children every year. If you remind them of that, they will be very glad to welcome whatever the library can bring to their efforts.

Ten Minutes a Week for Training

Here are some problem situations you might use in training sessions with staff. The first four are meant to refresh workers on the library's standard coping procedures. The fifth is a case which should provoke discussion about how a library staff should handle a situation with sexual overtones involving the potential safety of a child.

1. A patron comes to the desk and reports that a man in the nonfiction stacks has just exposed himself to her. "Oh yeah, him," says your page, who has overheard the patron report. "Don't worry. He does that all the time."

2. In the children's room you observe a young man who doesn't seem to be after any books, but is spending a lot of time moving up and down the stack aisles. You ask if you can help him find something, and he says no. Since Brownie Scout Troop 36 is due to arrive for a "class visit" in fifteen minutes, and you are not going to be able to keep an eye on him for much longer, what should you do?

3. A library patron comes to the main desk and reports that she is being stared at by a scruffy looking guy who she says is "pretending to read." She says she has moved twice, but he keeps following her. You ask her to come and point him out for you. She refuses, saying she just wants you to know what kind of people hang around in the library. What do you do?

4. You are working at the main desk when a man storms into the library and shouts at you, "Where's the *1*#$%x*1*#$% •& who tried to attack my daughter! What kind of place is this that you can't even protect little girls from being harassed by monsters. You just sit here and read books all day, am I right?" This is the first you have heard of the incident, although you faintly remember the man as the father of one of your after-school regulars. How should this situation be handled?

5. The branch has several latchkey children, including an eight year old girl who frightens you with her obvious need and desire for physical affection. You don't know what is going on at her home, but you are disturbed by the way she will talk with anyone, male or female, who shows any kindness to her. Yesterday you saw her being "petted" by a man whom you are sure she doesn't know. You stopped that incident by distracting the child, but now you wonder what you should do to find a permanent resolution to a situation you are sure is leading to some sort of disaster.

NOTES

1. The definitions of deviant behavior used in this chapter are taken from the American Psychiatric Association. *Diagnostic and Statistical Manual of Mental Disorders*, Third Edition, Revised. Washington, D.C.: American Psychiatric Association, 1987.

2. Ibid., p. 285.

3. Ibid., p. 283.

4. Ibid., p. 284.

5. Laning, Kenneth V. "Child Molesters: A Behavioral Analysis for Law Enforcement Officers Investigating Cases of Child Sexual Exploitation." April 1987, in U.S. Department of Justice, Federal Bureau of Investigation. *Deviant and Criminal Sexuality*. Quantico, Virginia: National Center for the Analysis of Violent Crime, 1991.

6. The author is extremely grateful to Meredith Pierce and the staff of the Alachua County Library for permission to quote Ms. Pierce extensively on an incident which caused her much pain and anxiety.

Quotations in this chapter are based on the following telephone interviews with the author: Linda Luke, Alachua County Library, Gainesville, Florida, September 1, 1992; Carole Hildebrand, director, Eugene (Oregon) Public Library, September 1, 1992; Meredith Pierce, Alachua County Library, Gainesville, Florida, September 1, 1992.

6. "It's Free and It's Safe" — Handling Problems with Latchkey Children

I was on an airplane flying from Hartford to Chicago one day, compressed into one of those ever-shrinking three-seat rows, when I was saved from existential misery by the discovery that my seatmates — a married couple — were strong supporters of their local county public library. She taught first grade in the local schools, and he, a retired school principal, was the chair of the local library commission.

Since we all came from the same state, we managed to fill the hours of involuntary physical proximity with a lively discussion of automation system installations, plans for their new library building, and the recent sins of the parsimonious state legislature. Their county is a very rural one (33,000 people in more than 1,000 square miles), so I was surprised when one of them remarked that a reason they were so desperate for a new building was the fact that mobs of elementary schoolkids flooded the existing library every afternoon after school.

"You mean you have a problem with latchkey children," I said.

"Well," one said, "I don't know if I'd call it a problem, exactly, but we do have a lot of kids with no place to go when school gets out, so they come to the library. Child care isn't any better in rural areas than it is in downtown Los Angeles, you know. In fact, it's probably better in L.A. where at least they have some resources."

"Latchkey" children — subteens whose parents require them to spend significant time at the public library after school in lieu of daycare — and the problems they create for libraries, have been a hot issue at library conferences and in the library press since the early 1980s. While after school use by kids is not exactly new (when did any of us go to the public library except after school?), the number of parents relying on the library to provide a safe refuge for their children (whether the kids like it or not) has definitely increased.

One part of the latchkey situation presents itself merely as a specialized component of the overall task of providing library services to children, and this chapter reflects that fact at certain points of analysis and suggestion: the information needs of latchkey kids are no different from those of other children. And library rules regarding behavior of latchkey kids are the same rules that apply to behavior of, say, children turned loose in the building by a parent who then becomes unresponsively absorbed in personal reading, or kids who come to the library unaccompanied because their parents, at home, trust them to do the right thing when they get there.

But in its larger implications, the latchkey problem extends well beyond the routine of children's services. Security, protection, and emergency medical potentials related to latchkey kids are particularly acute and troublesome. So are the overcrowding, abuse of facilities, and impossible demands on staff resulting from the increase in these rootless afternoon youngsters.

Changes in society and the economy have brought us this problem. Politicians who say that it's not the role of government or the schools to provide daycare, or that there aren't enough resources, need to take cognizance of a painful fact: a hidden, increasingly stressful part of most library budgets and staff workdays is being devoted to the afternoon supervision of children whose parents can't find or can't afford other options, and who know that the library is both free and safe.

By the end of 1992 there were two good books (one is actually a 76-page "position paper") on the subject, and they both should be consulted by any library staff which believes it has a latchkey problem. The position paper is *"Latchkey Children" in the Public Library*, prepared in 1988 by the Service to Children Committee of ALA's Public Library Association.[1] The book is Frances Smardo Dowd's *Latchkey Children in the Library and Community*, published by Oryx Press in 1991.[2]

Both sources, as well as a variety of periodical articles in library and popular literature, identify changing demographic factors as the principal reason why there are more latchkey children than there used to be. These factors include more women in the workforce, more single-parent households, fewer adults available to care for children in their neighborhoods, lack of accessible and affordable child care, and an increase in the number of homeless families with children.

The fact that parents regard the library as a suitable place for their children to spend after-school hours is, of course, to some extent a compliment. After all these years of librarians' work to provide a warm and welcoming atmosphere, offering important intellectual resources for children, many parents have gotten the message.

But, to the extent that the public library is regarded as the community's dumping ground for the latest social problem no one wants to spend the money to solve (including the use of libraries as day centers for street people), it is infuriating. It is so maddening, in fact, that it is easy to relish the acerbic words of one of the library world's more opinionated columnists, Herb White: "Hospitals also serve children; why don't the kids go there after school? Certainly in part because hospitals won't have them.... Because we have allowed ourselves to be so trivialized, the library can be seen simply as a handy place to come in out of the rain."[3]

But "trivialized" is the wrong word. Cutting through the rhetoric, the angst, and perhaps a tendency to feel sorry for ourselves, let's try, if we can, to get to the heart of the matter.

All children have information needs. Some children have shelter needs outside the home. The library's job is to meet the information needs. It is not the library's job to provide shelter. But taking those needs apart can be very difficult. Many libraries find themselves forced to shelter school-aged youngsters for part of every day in order to meet their information needs. Almost the only way to prevent parents from imposing shelter demands on libraries is to ban all children between the ages of six and twelve from 2:30 to 5:30 p.m. on weekdays. One's suspicion is that if a library actually announced it couldn't handle the demands being placed on it, and closed during the after-school hours, the community would quickly manage to find an alternative child care solution.

I believe that the dimensions of most libraries' latchkey problems depend on the size of their staff budgets, and the amount of space in their buildings. Now honestly, isn't it true? If my library had enough money to hire professional librarians and support staff at a ratio of one for every seven or eight kids hanging around in the afternoon, *and* we had enough space to give every child a chair, a table, a cubby to keep a lunch box, and room on the floor for creative lying around, would we still regard latchkey kids as a problem?

I bet we wouldn't. We'd be too busy thinking up just the right book for Manuel to read, or finding someone to help Marcia with her arithmetic. We'd be looking forward, as the kids are, to the next chapter in whatever book we're reading aloud. We wouldn't care a whit whether combined information and shelter services in the after-noons for youngsters is a proper function of the public library.

But this is a fantasy, of course. None of us have that kind of money, not even the libraries with successful latchkey programs. Financial reality forces us to limit our services. It is what we agree those latchkey limits should be, and how we go about enforcing them, that is the real question. And making sensible "limit" decisions is only possible when a library has engaged in a serious planning process.

Who Are the Latchkey Children?

"Latchkey Children" in the Public Library identifies three main categories of children using the library after school:

> those who choose to frequent the public library because of personal, natural affinities for the library environment;

> those who live nearby and go to the library because it is preferable to being at home alone after school;

> those children who are instructed to use the library as a shelter by parents and guardians who are unable to provide alternative care for them.[4]

It goes on to quote the San Marino, California, library's definition:

> A Library Latchkey child is one who on a regular basis is required by his/her parent or guardian to remain at the public library for extended periods of time after school in lieu of day care. "Regular basis" is defined as three or more days per week. "Extended period" is defined as two or more hours per day.[5]

Please note the modifier "library" associated with the word "latch-key." The children who come to the library are only a fraction of those who spend their after-school hours unsupervised. The rest are at home alone, on the street, hanging around at the shopping mall, at the houses of friends (where they also may be unsupervised), and who knows where else, courting trouble in the cracks between schools and the general society which apparently does not care about their situation.

Another word libraries use to describe these kids is "unattended," meaning unattended by parents or guardians. But unattended children must be divided by age.

Preschoolers left without parental supervision present special problems: they are not old enough to be left alone at the library, any more than they are old enough to be left alone at home. Many libraries have therefore adopted rules which require parents or guardians to stay with their children when they are in the library.

Some go on to define the minimum age the "guardian" or caregiver must be in order to prevent underage siblings from bringing their charges to the library and then leaving them in the staff's care. Babysitting sisters and brothers who are too young for the job (regardless of what the cultural traditions of their families may be), become the source of problems for staff, forcing intervention when inappropriate or abusive behavior develops.

Both the PLA policy paper and most working children's librarians urge swift action when parents disobey the "unattended" rule with very young children: find the parents and tell them directly that they may not leave their preschooler alone in the children's room or anywhere else in the library.

Older children are "unattended" when their parents have left them to find books or whatever for themselves while the parents do other errands or use the adult collection. They are not a problem until their behavior interferes with other people's rights to use the library.

And there are the true latchkey kids who meet the San Marino definition.

Service Roles and Policies

The policy arguments libraries get into as they confront the "latchkey problem" are a classic example of failure to define service roles and set clear boundaries around them. This was one of Herb White's messages in the article featuring his famous suggestion that kids could go to hospitals after school. Too often we have shouldered the burden of a community problem, simply because it has been thrust upon us, instead of saying loudly and clearly, "No, we are **not** in the child shelter business, and we are not going to be everybody's free after-school child care facility."

The thrust of most documents being written by American Library Association committees and divisions is that every public library is different, and endeavors to serve a different community. National standards are inappropriate in making plans and designing services. The local library needs to study its community to find out its characteristics, its desires, and its information needs. Then the library should assess which of those needs it can try to meet.

The model developed by the Public Library Association for conducting this planning process requires a library to define service roles for itself, and orient its programs and collections toward those roles.[6] This concept flows from the observation that the demands for service from public libraries are exceedingly diverse, very complex, and frequently conflicting. Libraries traditionally have tried to be all things to all people. But this is an impossible task, and thus public libraries should choose and limit their efforts to service roles that match their resources with the unique needs of their communities.

The PLA publication *Planning and Role Setting for Public Libraries* lists three operations roles which relate directly to services to children: Formal Education Support Center, Independent Learning Center, and Preschoolers' Door to Learning. But there are other options (including hybrids a library might devise for itself). If a public library has decided that its primary role is to be a research center, it is not likely to be in a position to do very much with kids under college age, and it should say so in its policy statement.

If, on the other hand, the library sees itself as an Education Support Center, it will adopt policies defining the responsibilities of parents, but will perforce acknowledge that it is going to have programs which meet the needs of latchkey kids along with other children. Stating (and posting) those parental responsibilities are important, but are only one part of the library's overall policy regarding services to children.

If a public library does define a role for itself in children's services, it then must go on to identify the details of childrens' information needs, and it must design programs to meet them. The library can and should be assisted in this process by other community groups serving children: the schools, the voluntary service agencies targeting families and children, the boys' and girls' clubs, scout organizations, and the like.

This process of role definition, and matching of resources and programs, is a golden opportunity for library staffs (and boards) to involve other provider agencies, and politicians too, in explicating real needs, and understanding what the library can and cannot do to meet them. The object is to get the community to agree that the problem requires a collective response.

Components of a Latchkey Policy

"Latchkey Children" in the Public Library advises that a library's latchkey policy have an introduction which clarifies needs, a statement of the policy itself, a problem definition, and procedures for staff. I don't quite understand this order — surely policies flow from the problem, not the reverse. But let's not quibble over format. Whatever model the library uses, the document which is the basis for staff work and public understanding of the library's response to the needs of children unattended after school should contain:

- a clear and positive statement of what the library's services to school aged youngsters will be, and
- a clear and positive statement of what the responsibilities of parents must be.

The policy will also have procedures appended, although these might more usefully reside in the larger staff "problem situations" manual.

Problems and Procedures to Help Handle Latchkey Kids

Obviously, it is the children who meet the San Marino definition who cause problems, among other reasons because of the involuntary nature of their presence. Kids who want to be at the library are our favorite patrons. And those who choose us over other alternatives will probably do okay most of the time.

It is those children who are sent to the library for daycare who most often create difficulties for underfunded and understaffed public libraries.

There seem to be four major problems created by school-age latchkey kids: liability, child security, disruptive behavior, and inappropriate use. The last two in particular are exacerbated by the problem of too little space.

Library Liability

Here are some of my worst library latchkey fantasies: that a child will be snatched from the library steps and subsequently molested by a sexual deviant. Or that a seven year old will trip and crack her head on the lobby floor: she is unconscious, we've called for emergency help, and no one knows how to reach her parent. Or that a child will be kidnapped from the children's room by a parent involved in a custody fight, and the library will be sued by the other parent. Are libraries legally responsible (i.e., liable) for the physical safety of kids who use them after school?

As *"Latchkey Children" in the Public Library* points out, the legal answer is, as usual, murky. We know that "the public library as an institution does not have the legal 'provision of care' responsibilities mandated for schools."[7] And we know that a library staff member should never, ever drive a child home in his or her own car. But aside from these two rules, no legal issues are certain or uniform in all states or localities.

The library's best protection from legal liability, although **not** from lawsuits (which litigious people can and will file for purely arbitrary reasons) are statements of responsibility and behavior rules for parents and children written with the same care as those written for other users (see Chapter 1). Furthermore,

> An "unattended children" policy cannot guarantee that public library staff will not be subpoenaed to appear as witnesses in child custody hearings, should a child be taken by the non-custodial parent from library property. Nor are staff guaranteed exemption from being queried by police or subpoenaed to repeat children's verbal confidences that are later seen as useful in child abuse and/or neglect hearings. Confidentiality in the library sense, with few exceptions, still only means legally that circulation records are protected.[8]

The library staff's best approach to the liability issue is to consult with local counsel and appropriate risk managers when they formulate their policies regarding children. And if these advisers (harassed, perhaps, by the cost of "deep pocket" lawsuits and self-insurance premiums) give advice which is too conservative to allow the library to do its job, then try getting more guidance (re other case law, for example) from ALA's Association for Library Service to Children and the PLA Service to Children Committee.

Security

The security issue arises when a parent has not picked up a child by the time the library closes. Or suppose there is a community disaster or a fire which forces the building to be evacuated and closed. A library needs to establish a procedure for what it is going to do when this happens, so that staff are not left to make up solutions on the spot. And the procedure needs to take into account the age of the child and the location of the library.

Library staff members are not going to be willing to abandon a seven year old on the front steps on a winter evening at 6 p.m. But leaving a twelve year old to his or her own devices is a bit more acceptable, depending on the library's neighborhood, of course. Many libraries instruct staff to take abandoned children to the local police station, or to call the police for a pick up. This doesn't work, however, if the library branch is in a rural area, the sheriff is miles away, and the patrol will thus be a long time in coming. One solution is for the rural branch manager to work out an "abandoned child" arrangement with whatever other government agency is available—for example, the local fire department.

We all know that disasters happen to adults: a terrible accident has blocked traffic for hours and miles, the bus is late, the office caught on fire. Therefore compassion and sympathy should certainly be our attitude. But the parent who gets into this kind of mess, and can't make it to the library by closing time, is forcing the library staff to pay a penalty for the parent's decision to use the library for shelter services. The parent should not be using the library in that way, and he or she should be confronted with the truth, using language such as "child abandonment" or "child neglect" which will make the mistake crystal clear.

Disruptive Behavior and Inappropriate Use

The philosophy behind making behavior rules for kids should be the same as for adults: no one has the right to interfere with anyone else's right to use the library. And in terms of that philosophy, it doesn't much matter whether children are with a parent or in the library on their own.

In either case kids can behave beautifully, or like monsters. The library staff needs to think through what its space will accommodate, and what other users can tolerate. For example, a children's room in the basement or isolated on the second floor can probably take more noise than one which is adjacent to the main adult reference area. And the staff of a severely overcrowded facility is obviously going to be less tolerant of collective homework doing or other talking than one with a lot of space.

Young people, especially as they reach sixth grade, are increasingly likely to use the "adult" areas of the library too, where their behavior may need to conform to more stringent rules against talking, snapping bubble gum, and generally annoying other people. Judith Drescher, at the Memphis–Shelby County Library and Information Center, reports that the largest number of problem situations her staff encounters at the headquarters library are complaints from adults about the presence and behavior of kids. It is not that the kids are bad, so much as that there are a lot of them, after school, in a too-small space.

Among other things, the Memphis staff tries to advise adults of when the library is less likely to be a youth haven — for instance, in the morning, while kids are in school.

Here is how the Santa Clara County (California) Library states its behavior rules for young users:

> Appropriate activities include: doing homework, writing reports, researching, browsing for books, thinking, daydreaming, and reading. If games, puzzles, or listening tables are available, they are to be used quietly so as not to disturb others.

> Inappropriate activities include: running, throwing, eating, loud or abusive talking, fighting, moving furniture, excessive socializing, or any other activities which disrupt the library. Vandalism will not be tolerated.[9]

And of course, as with all rule enforcement, success is based on the ability to be flexible. The Santa Cruz Library System has a small branch in the redwoods of the coastal mountains. The coach at the local high school likes to assign his track team to a five mile training run in which the halfway point is the branch. The runners pant up the steps and into the library (which is only one room), where they must get a library stamp on the back of their hand from the desk worker to prove they did the whole run. Then they are out the door on the back-to-school leg. As after-school support for local kids, I think this one has a certain charm, even if the behavior does violate several standard library rules (no running, no heavy breathing), and also interferes with the right of anyone standing at the circulation desk to complete a book checkout while the track team is visiting.

Procedures for handling all these problems need to be developed with the participation of the staff doing the job. Appendix F has an example of both policy and procedures from the Duluth (Minnesota) Public Library.

Getting the Message Out

Having gone to the trouble of thinking through the library's response to the issue of library latchkey services, as well as other services to children and young adults, the library's next task is to inform the public about it. It is especially necessary to tell parents about the policy and program. Here are some ideas for doing that.

1. **Send Home a Letter**. Many libraries require a parental signature on a child's borrower card application, and many don't. In either case, a youngster getting a library card creates an ideal opportunity for the staff to tell parents about the library's services to children, and its rules. This can be done via a letter mailed to the parent or guardian at the child's home address, or by handing it to the parent on the spot. Included in the letter should be a statement of parental responsibility when the child is in the library, and (if appropriate) the library's refusal to provide ongoing shelter services.

2. **Put Out a Leaflet**. Keep on hand a standard flyer describing services to children and listing rules. This can be given to violators, or to anyone who asks.

3. **Post the Unattended Child Rule**. Regardless of where the library stands in the posting rules debate (see Chapter 1), it should at

least post the rule about how parents must accompany their children. And, it should post it in the adult areas of the library, as well as in the children's room.

4. **Try to Interest the Media.** The best kind of coverage is a long feature article and a television story about library efforts to meet the information needs of school-age children, including those left on their own after school. If stories like these can't be finagled, try to get the local press interested in the larger problem. Produce other service providers for a joint press conference. Get the mayor to declare a Latchkey Children Day. The point in this is to put across the message that after-school care is a community-wide responsibility. The library is do-ing its part, but it can't carry the whole burden, and so forth.

5. **Work with the Local Schools.** Sure, sure, you're thinking. We always want to work with them, but they never want to work with us, except of course when a teacher wants to bring a class to visit, or they've closed the school media center in the latest budget crunch, and we're expected to pick up the slack. And why can't they let us know when they assign a whole class to a topic such as astrobiology, about which we have only three books, all of which were checked out by the early birds.

Frankly, I don't have a great deal of sympathy for the trials and tribulations of school staffs—especially for those staffers who obviously don't have any sympathy for the lot of the working librarian. Why is it, for example, that school in the United States ends at 2:30 or 3 in the afternoon? In Europe and Japan children go to school until 5 p.m. or later. But this is a personal prejudice, no doubt informed by the fact that I have never been a teacher, and by my knowledge that we wouldn't have a "latchkey problem," library or otherwise, if the public schools were organized as full day operations.

Ignoring such bias, the number one priority in working with the schools, whether it is meeting the needs of their teachers, or trying to develop a community response to the latchkey problem, is to make the dimensions (and limits) of public library service clear, and stick to the rules we make to express those limits. If we say an appointment is required for a class visit, then we should refuse to provide special services to a teacher and her twenty students who turn up without one. And we should report habitual offenders (a teacher who does this more than once) to the school principal. If we don't do this, neither the schools nor anyone else is going to take our parental responsibility and other rules seriously.

The second step is to get a little back from the schools, such as space for articles in the P.T.A. newsletter, and a message home for every child at the beginning of each new school year. The letter can be the same as the one delivered when children apply for borrower cards: a welcome to the public library, a description of library services, an explanation of the library rules, and a clear statement of the library's latchkey policy.

Latchkey Programs That Work

Frances Smardo Dowd's book, *Latchkey Children in the Library and Community*, offers descriptions of several successful programs, as well as a comprehensive list of latchkey organizations and agencies, and an excellent annotated bibliography. The PLA work, *"Latchkey Children" in the Public Library*, summarizes the various types of programs offered—drop-in centers, clubs, phone help lines, and the like. And Linda Rome's April 1990 article in *Wilson Library Bulletin* describes a variety of library efforts, large and small, in Ohio.[10]

The most interesting thing about all these programs is their diversity. They range from bookmobile service at private care centers to the "Grandparents and Books" program at the Los Angeles Public Library, which seeks to link lonely older people with kids in need of after-school support. Homework centers, often assisted by volunteers, are a popular and successful program. Frequency ranges from regular daily service to once-a-week special programs. Librarians have coped by opening their meeting rooms and adding vending machines in the lobby so kids have access to snacks.

Many library staffs, especially those from the larger library systems, have taken on the advocacy function, endeavoring to organize community-wide responses at the same time that they run after-school programs in their own facilities. The need to find services for latchkey children is an excellent example of the kind of institutional networking all public libraries are increasingly required to do.

Ten Minutes a Week for Training

Any children's staff endeavoring to serve library latchkey kids is surely doing its own planning and training exercises on the special issues of how to "do it good." It is important to remember, though, that the adult services staff also interacts with kids, and may need special coaching in how to do this effectively. Here are some questions and problem examples which might be used to provoke a discussion aimed at consciousness raising and training. Remember that these training exercises are aimed too at reminding staff of what your library's standard rules are.

1. Mrs. Jones storms up to the adult reference desk and demands that you "do something" about that group of giggly girls over in the corner. What do you say and do?
2. It is 6 p.m. and closing time. It is also raining and dark. Michael, who is eleven, is still hanging around at the front entrance. You ask how he is going to get home, and he says his dad is picking him up. "What time?" you ask. "Oh, I guess about five," says Michael. What do you do?
3. "Mrs.," says a child approaching you at the desk. "Nancy is being sick awful bad in the bathroom." You investigate and find that indeed Nancy is vomiting and probably has a fever. And yes, she is on her own at the library. Her mother is at work, and her dad is not at home either. What's next?
4. Again and again the children's room staff have told Mrs. Smith that she cannot tell her youngsters to go to the library every day after school, and wait until she gets off work to pick them up. She says she is a single parent with no money and has no choice. The children are rarely troublesome, but keeping them occupied is requiring a lot of staff attention. What are the staff's options here?
5. The mayor (who is a reliable library supporter, but at the moment is running in a hard-fought race for reelection) is speaking at a candidates' forum. In response to a question, she suggests that parents who can't afford after school care for their youngsters send their kids to the public library. "It's free," she says, "You're already paying for it. And it's safe." What should the director do?

NOTES

1. *"Latchkey Children" in the Public Library: A Position Paper*. Chicago: Prepared by the Service to Children Committee of the Public Library Association in Collaboration with the Library Service to Children with Special Needs Committee of the Association for Library Service to Children, May 1988.

2. Dowd, Frances Smardo. *Latchkey Children in the Library and Community*. Phoenix, Ariz.: Oryx Press, 1991.

3. White, Herbert S. "Pseudo-Libraries and Semi-Teachers." Part 1. *American Libraries*, Vol. 21, No. 2, February 1990, p. 106.

4. *"Latchkey Children" in the Public Library: A Position Paper*, p. 12.

5. Ibid., p. 12.

6. McClure, Charles R., et al. *Planning and Role Setting for Public Libraries — a Manual of Options and Procedures*. Chicago: American Library Association, 1987.

7. *"Latchkey Children" in the Public Library*, p. 16.

8. Ibid., p. 17.

9. Santa Clara (Calif.) County Library. "Santa Clara County Library Procedures Manual," April 1, 1984. Part A, Section 501.1, B.1 & B.2.

10. Rome, Linda. "Service to Latchkey Kids and the Public Library — Dealing with the Real Issues." *Wilson Library Bulletin*: 64: April 1990, pp. 34–37, 126.

7. Did You Know This Book Is About Witchcraft?

Here are extracts from a story which ran on the Associated Press wire service September 8, 1992:

KIDS' BOOK ABOUT GAY DAD CREATES UPROAR

Goldsboro, N.C. (AP) When a child pulled "Daddy's Roommate" from a shelf in the kids' library, he began a conflict that touched on censorship, homosexuality, divorce and who chooses books for the library.

"Daddy's Roommate" [by Michael Willhoite] uses simple terms and illustrations — showing Daddy and his roommate, Frank, eating, working and sleeping together — to tell the story of a gay, divorced father. . . .

"It's not an issue of censorship. . . . This is plain common sense," said Dr. Joseph Ponzi, a pediatrician who wants the book out of the children's library. "This book is fairly offensive to 98 percent of parents with kids."

It all started when one of Joe and Karen Grant's children plucked the book from the "easy reading" section of the children's library. The Grants filed a formal complaint. After a review, [the library director] moved the book to a section of the children's library dealing with juvenile social issues.[1]

As the librarians in Goldsboro surely know — like their colleagues in Roswell, New Mexico, Springfield, Oregon, and other places where the book was also challenged — the furor over *Daddy's Roommate* has all the elements of a classic censorship case, 1990s style. The book focuses on one of the most controversial issues of the sexual revolution. It also deals with parent/child relationships (always an emotional subject). And so the range of complainants extended beyond those who oppose homosexuality per se, or discussions of any sort of sexuality in library collections, to include persons who apparently believe that "censorship" is what other misguided people do, while they act on the basis of common sense.

Attempts to censor library materials are on the rise, although the actual numbers depend upon who is doing the counting. It is certainly true that complaints about materials go in waves, and despite the wide range of responses to books such as *Daddy's Roommate*, the wave of the early nineties is mainly from the religious right.

Evolving along with the world we live in, the advice from the American Library Association's Office of Intellectual Freedom about policies and procedures for handling attempts at book censorship has changed a bit over the years.

It used to be that all questions from the public about materials were automatically assumed to be hostile and challenging. The response forms libraries kept on hand for these emergencies had names such as "Materials Reconsideration Request." The assumption was always that the patron wanted the book removed. The burden of the form (aside from bibliographic identification of the item) was finding out whether the patron represented him or herself, or (oh no, now we're in for trouble) an *Organization*.

These days, the attitude isn't so automatically defensive. It is not so much that librarians are agreeing to remove materials as that they have begun to recognize that many people who challenge a title really only want to talk with someone about it.

Experience shows that there are significantly different types of complaints in this category of librarians' woes. Publicity goes to the ideologues: individuals and organizations demanding that a book be removed or its location in the collection changed, or that censors should scour our public and school library collections of any materials at variance with their own beliefs.

But many of the people who file such complaints (lots of libraries now take these on "comment forms") are like the man who objected to a cassette tape of ghost stories which had scared the dickens out of his five year old. The cassette package was clearly marked, "Ages Nine Years Old and Up," and what the man really wanted to talk about was how to choose recorded stories and books for his little boy.

A traditional review of the complaint would have involved looking up the reviews and citing them in a letter explaining the *Library Bill of Rights* and why this specific item met various library selection criteria. And all that work would have missed the point.

But the librarian responding to the complaint form took a better tack. First, she called the parent, learned that the real problem was the age of the child, and that what the father needed was advice. They had an interesting conversation about what kids of five like to read and hear, and both were happy. The library "closed the case" with the staff person writing the patron a short letter saying she had been glad to talk with him.

Library procedures for handling complaints or questions about materials need to address both levels of challenge: attempts to "purify" the collection, and the more mundane concerns of worried library users which perhaps can be addressed by explanation or conversation. Procedures also should allow for the fact that not every professional librarian selecting materials is available to talk to the public every minute of the day, and that therefore the commenting patron's first encounter may well be with a member of the library's support staff. But before creating these procedures, the library needs to make sure it has its basic principles and policies in place and in writing.

Creating an Environment of Intellectual Freedom

The American Library Association's Office of Intellectual Freedom, as well as the intellectual freedom committees of ALA and the state library associations, all provide solid guidance to libraries in creating what they call "environments of intellectual freedom" (i.e., free speech). The ALA's *Intellectual Freedom Manual*, 4th edition, is a truly comprehensive resource which should be on the shelves of every library in the United States.[2] Based on those references, this chapter summarizes some basic groundwork any library must do, and then gets on to its major focus—enabling staff to handle complaints or questions about library materials.

First you need to get your intellectual freedom ducks in order, as it were, by creating a comprehensive materials selection, or collection development, statement (also called a program, policy, or plan). The *Intellectual Freedom Manual* suggests that this document should reflect the library's investigation of its community and its needs, and the library's objectives, geographic environment, and the current collection.

But the basic point is to write it, make it official. The statement should be organized in two parts. Part One is the policies: what and why the library does what it does. Part Two contains procedures: how the library does it. The *Manual* makes the point that even the smallest public library needs to take the time and trouble to get this information written down—otherwise, it can make only the poorest of defenses against challenges.

The policy part of the statement sets out the library's understanding of its institutional mission and objectives, and the commitment of its governing authority and staff to the principles of the *Library Bill of Rights* (see Appendix A).

This section also needs to specify the objectives of the library's collection (what user needs is the collection endeavoring to meet?), who is responsible for selection (e.g., the director, who delegates to the professional staff), and the criteria the staff will use in making selections (artistic or literary excellence, appropriateness to level of user, authenticity, interest, cost, review recommendations, and so forth).

Finally, the policy statement should tell patrons how the library handles controversial material, starting with the governing authority's commitment to the *Library Bill of Rights* and its supporting Interpretations. Two of the Interpretations (Exhibits and Displays and Meeting Rooms) are also contained in Appendices A and B. But there are at least five additional Interpretations which relate directly to selection of library materials, and seven more which concern collection access. The latter in particular include important principles about information for children. All these documents are printed and explained in the *Intellectual Freedom Manual*.

Part Two of the Materials Selection Statement should contain specific information about how the library implements the policies set out in Part One: what selection aids the staff will use, how it will handle gifts, procedures for managing special collections, and collection maintenance issues—review of existing materials, weeding, and the like.

Part Two should also include a detailed explanation of how the library will handle challenges to library materials: the name of the form the patron fills out, what the staff person who receives the form does with it, which professional library position handles the comment, the appeals process, and so forth. Typical sequences of events are outlined in the sample procedures and policies in Appendix F.

The *Intellectual Freedom Manual* devotes a whole chapter to the ins and outs of conducting this process properly and productively. One particularly important point is that the process should be objective, fair, honest, and open.

> The review procedure, including the written questionnaire [materials comment form], should be designed not only as a defense against potential censors, but also as a means to facilitate constructive dialogue. While these procedures do offer the library a defense against arbitrary attacks, they should never be permitted to degenerate into a bureaucratic smokescreen. In a word, the library should welcome constructive input even as it maintains firm barriers to censorship.[3]

The materials selection statement which results from including all these elements is inevitably long and complex. That's why I am convinced that the *Library Bill of Rights* should be the lead document, always cited first, in any question about selection of materials. Its principles are basic, it has a good title, and it is shorter:

> Books and other library resources should be provided for the interest, information, and enlightenment of all people of the community the library serves. . . .

> Libraries should provide materials and information representing all points of view on current and historical issues. Materials should not be proscribed or removed because of partisan or doctrinal disapproval.[4]

Handling Comments About Materials — The First Round

So we all read the *Intellectual Freedom Manual,* and follow its advice about devising a process for handling complaints. And then we come up against the fact that 99 percent of the situations invoking these carefully crafted procedures end before they ever reach the library director, let alone the library board. That's why it is so important to train all staff in how to respond.

A very wise person once observed that a lot of time is wasted answering questions which were never asked. The trick in handling a question about library materials is to find out what the person really wants to know: why did the library select this particular book or other item? Why does the library buy books on this subject? Why is this book shelved in the "easy reader" section of the children's room? Does the library have any other books by this author? There are a hundred other variations on the theme.

Like the pediatrician in Goldsboro, North Carolina, most people (other than zealots) who raise questions about a book or other item don't think of themselves as censors and they don't believe in censorship. "Censorship" is a bad word in most Americans' vocabulary — a fact which should reassure any library worker responding to such a challenge. Most "censors" simply don't like a specific item, and want to be able to tell somebody (like a library staff person) what they think about that terrible book/magazine/video.

As one librarian put it, "Dealing with book complaints is a *service* we provide the public." And, added another, it is a service we should train our staffs to do as well as any other we provide.

Monroe County (Michigan) Library Director Gordon Conable (who was also the 1992-1993 president of the Freedom to Read Foundation) suggests that if you think of a book query as a request for service, instead of a complaint, it is a lot less paralyzing. Handling it requires the same skills as those used in a reference interview to extract the real question from the patron: active listening and open-ended questioning.

Doing it well also requires practice. That's why it is very important to take the time at regular staff meetings to role-play encounters between public desk workers and patrons asking questions. See the "Ten Minutes a Week for Training" section at the end of this chapter for some question ideas.

Here's an example of a conversation between a library user and a staff member, in which the staff member tries to use her training in active listening to handle the problem. Alas, however, the user is so concerned about her own point of view that she doesn't want to listen.

User arrives at Circulation Desk, displaying agitation.

STAFF: May I help you?

USER: (*Sighing*) I don't know. I just found . . . I don't know . . . I just can't *believe* I found this book here. It is so evil, I just can't, you know, it is *sinful*.

STAFF: You're upset about a book you've found on the library shelves?

USER: Yes! Are you aware that you have this book? I am *really* upset about this. It is about *witchcraft*. I don't think the library should have books like this!

STAFF: You object to this book being in the library collection, is that it?

USER: Well, I think witchcraft is evil. I don't think you should advocate it.

STAFF: Actually, having a book about a subject isn't *advocating* it. Our job is to provide information about everything, including different kinds of beliefs.

USER:	But surely you don't believe in witchcraft. That is *evil*.
STAFF:	The library has a policy for selecting books and all our other materials. It is called the *Library Bill of Rights*, and it says that the library's job is to provide materials and information presenting all points of view. I can give you a copy if you'd like to read it.
USER:	Well, that may be, but what I want to know is who bought this book. This is truly horrible. And it is frightening. It's the work of the devil, truly, and it is dangerous to have it.
STAFF:	The professional library staff selects all our materials, based on the *Library Bill of Rights* and our Collection Development Plan. If you want to know why the staff picked this particular book, you need to fill out this form. Here's a copy of the form and also a copy of the *Library Bill of Rights*.
USER:	No, I don't *want* to do one of your forms. I just want you to know I think this is an outrageous book to have on the shelves, where young children can see it. Have you read it? Do you realize what it advocates?
STAFF:	The staff will be interested to hear your comments on the book, and whoever is responsible for that part of the collection will call you to talk about it, and send you a letter too. But you *do* have to fill out the form saying which book it is, and giving your name, address, and phone number if you want them to consider your opinion.
USER:	Well, all right. I *do* want to *talk* with someone about this. I think you really need to be careful about the books you have.
STAFF:	Here's the Comment Form. I'll make sure the right librarian gets it, and she'll call you. Are you at home during the day, or is the evening better?

The staff's objective in handling a complaint like this one is to ensure that the person making the comment gets the chance to talk out what she or he thinks. If the patron can't do it right then, she needs to give enough information so that a member of the professional staff can get back to her. Best would be a Comment Form, but in a pinch, the name and phone number will do. The patron also needs to be given a brief rendition of the library's procedures for selecting materials, and for handling complaints about them.

The librarian who follows up on this kind of query will telephone the patron, talk about the question or complaint, and if the patron hasn't already filled out a Comment Form making an "official" comment or complaint, send her one. The librarian would write a response letter which includes a restatement of the *Library Bill of Rights* and other appropriate principles, information on the place the item has in the library's collection development plan, and citations of reviews used when the item was originally evaluated. The letter would also tell the patron what to do next if she wishes to take the matter further. The next step is usually an appeal to the library director.

Good record keeping is essential in this process. A copy of the original Comment Form, as well as the staff response letter or phone call notes should immediately be placed in a central file, where it is accessible to the director or other staff who may need it if the patron isn't satisfied.

Confronting a Censorship Attempt

As it turned out, the woman who despised the witchcraft book got her letter from the selection librarian, and followed up with an appeal to the library director, who also defended the book selection. So the unhappy patron consulted with her minister, and they decided to file a complaint with the library board, demanding a formal hearing.

When this kind of situation develops, a library director should make no bones about the fact that what's being confronted is an attempt to censor the library's collection. Don't try to clothe the issue in less pejorative terms. Regardless of how "nice" or "flaky" or "religious" the people making the challenge may be, the issue is censorship, and you must call it that. This is a battle which also is probably going to be fought in the pages of the local newspaper, so it is crucial that the library and its governing authority be proactive, not reactive, to the situation.

Among the very first things a director should do is to notify the intellectual freedom committee of the state library association or the American Library Association. The reason is the light these groups may be able to shed on the organization, if there is one, mounting the challenge — what their past practice has been, the reputation of their attorneys, their success rate, comparable cases, and the like. It is a tried and true rule of conflict: the more you know about your opponent, the better off you will be.

It is also smart to do two other things immediately. First, inform the staff of the pending censorship attempt, and what is being done about it. Do it by memo, or better, by meeting, so that everyone has a chance to ask questions, and rehearse responses to the public. Circulate the case file, so staff can read the selection librarian's response to the initial complaint. Remind staff not to get trapped into discussions of the book itself. The issue is the library's obligation to provide material representing all viewpoints.

Second, "refresh" the library governing authority, and especially the chair, on the principles of the *Library Bill of Rights* and its relevant Interpretations. Give them new copies. The board probably adopted this document years ago, and unless it has had a recent discussion of it, the members (and they may be new members) are not likely to be up-to-date on its implications.

Here's another tried and true rule of conflict: never let a politician be surprised by a question from the press. If the official doesn't know what the reporter is talking about, and embarrasses himself by saying the first thing that pops into his head (for example, "Gosh, we've got a book about that?") guess whose fault it will be?

Finally, building coalitions for intellectual freedom in advance is always good strategy. If you haven't had a chance to do that formally, at least prepare yourself by listing the groups in town whom you are pretty sure you can call on in an emergency. Not the least of these will be your own Friends of the Library group, who are as likely to be as well prepared as anyone to mount a quick information mobilization on the library's behalf. Virtually any other group in your community, from businesswomen's service organizations to the Central Labor Council, can be turned into allies if they are forcefully reminded that censorship of free speech at the library is the beginning of censorship of every-one's free speech.

Wading Ashore Always Looks Good

Working with the chair of the board, you should call in every chit you ever had with the working press, starting at the top with the local paper's editorial board, and going down through the ranks of individual reporters. Call them up, and ask for a meeting or an interview. Try to get them started into the issue from the standpoint that censorship at the library is the beginning of censorship of everyone's free speech, including the newspaper's.

In talking with reporters, stick to your basic points: libraries must provide material representing all viewpoints — this conflict is *not* about whether witchcraft is good or evil, it is about the right of the people to access to information in their public library. Avoid (if you can) castigating the person or group bringing the complaint, or impugning their motives.

Take the high moral and political ground, and don't let any challenger take it away from you: free speech, the First Amendment to the U.S. Constitution, freedom of thought as the American way, "In this country we are not afraid of ideas, but we are afraid of ignorance," and so forth.

Never hesitate to repeat what you have just said, no matter what you are asked—professional politicians do it all the time. Take a minute to think before you answer a question. Control the interview with silence when you aren't ready to talk, or if you don't want to answer.

An old reporter's trick is to sit quietly, looking expectant, and wait for you to get nervous and start filling the silence with talk. Turn the tables. Make the reporter ask the questions.

Radio talk and interview shows are very popular media in most communities, so try to get on as many of these as you can. But they do present special problems. Dead air time, i.e., silence, is the cardinal sin on the radio. Sometimes the interviewer will be so antsy that if you take a breath before you answer, he or she will jump in with another question. If you don't think you can be fluent on the radio (that is, talk while you are still thinking up an answer) find someone who can be. The most important thing is to *sound* competent, confident, and assured, as well as warm, friendly, and nonthreatening. Try pretending that the interviewer is your favorite aunt.

Local television is also problematic, primarily because the news shows deal in 20 second sound bites. This forces the reporters to talk in clichés, and gives you only a tiny moment to get across your message. One on-camera trick is to ignore the reporter's question, and say what you want. It doesn't matter, because the reporter is going to edit the story anyway; your object is to give her or him footage of you saying that the conflict is about the right of the people to access to information. Off camera you can explain the details to the reporter.

The typical television reporter is going to want to wave around a copy of the book about witchcraft, and lead with a sentence such as, "Should the Wicked Witch of the West be allowed in the public library? The Pure at Heart Organization says No. They are challenging a book called . . . ."

To a reporter, the most important part of the story is that a group has challenged a specific book. The reporter is going to focus on the group and what it says, unless you can find a means for taking the attention away from them. Try something visual, like a stack of all the books which have ever been banned, beginning with the classics. Talk about Nazis burning books in Germany. Use short sentences, but the most dramatic words you can think of. And don't worry about your hair: nearly everyone looks awful on television.

In case you are wondering how the *Daddy's Roommate* controversy in Goldsboro came out, here's what a city councilman—who is also a member of the library board—told the Associated Press reporter: "If that would be the worst thing we've got in this town, I'd be tickled to death. I have 12 grandchildren and I don't think their reading it would have any effect on them. People ought to be educated as to what is going on in this world."[5]

The Library Board voted 7 to 2 to keep the book in the juvenile social issues area of the collection. Alas, however, that reasonably satisfactory outcome was not so easily repeated in other communities where this book and others in the same series have been targeted for removal.

And it is extremely dismaying (not to say depressing) to realize that while certain groups are trying to censor the information libraries provide on important issues such as family diversity, the media has happily shifted its attention to whether libraries should buy *Sex* by Madonna, building up a fair amount of public interest in the process. Don't you love it when we have to defend the people's First Amendment right to read junk, and the library's need to buy it for them? Lucky is the library which has a collection development policy which provides clear guidance on whether it will or will not buy soft porn (and not very good soft porn at that) aimed at aggrandizing the career of a rock singer.

Ten Minutes a Week for Training

Here are some questions from library users which can be used for role playing practice by the staff.

1. I certainly think you should have a complete children's collection, but I worry. How do I know what my child is reading?
2. Why does the library keep copies of a book like *Mein Kampf*?
3. Are you aware that [pick your own title] contains information about abortion?
4. I really don't think you should let young people read novels like this one; it's about suicide.
5. Why doesn't the library put labels on the videos so we know which ones are bad?

NOTES

1. Associated Press Service, 09/10/92: **PM** — Daddy's Roommate, 0610. Children's Book About Gay Parent Creating Uproar. By Sue Price Wilson, Associated Press Writer.

2. American Library Association, Office for Intellectual Freedom, comp. *Intellectual Freedom Manual*. 4th ed. Chicago: American Library Association, 1992.

3. Ibid., p. 218.

4. American Library Association. *Library Bill of Rights*. Adopted June 18, 1948, amended February 2, 1961, June 27, 1967, and January 23, 1980, by the **ALA** Council.

5. Associated Press Service, 09/10/92.

Part III

Practical Advice

8. *Securing Our Buildings*

Did you know that among experienced library vandals a popular method for removing pages from books and periodicals is said to involve wet thread? You moisten the thread with spit and then lay it along the binding seam of the page you want. You close the book or magazine, hold the thread at one end, pull it from the other, and bingo! out comes the page.

This is a technique one of the experts described at an ALA Annual Conference program on building security, and his podium colleagues agreed with him. So of course I went home and tried it. I couldn't make it work, with either a paperback or an old *New Yorker*. I even used two different kinds of thread. Could it be that my saliva is not acidic enough? Or that I don't have the right wrist action? Whatever, as an observer pointed out (he couldn't get it to work either), if you wanted to mutilate magazines, wouldn't it be easier to use one of those little retractable single-blade razors encased in plastic, which are actually meant to be used for newspaper clipping? They are small enough to hide in the palm of the hand, and you don't have to worry about drooling.

The issue of materials mutilation came up at the ALA program in the context of what librarians should be looking for as they observe the users in their buildings. See someone with unexplained thread sticking out of their pocket (or mouth)? Watch out, because they could be after the new midsize car ratings in *Consumer Reports*.

This chapter is about what *else* librarians should be looking for—not just suspicious actions by patrons, but the physical arrangements inside our buildings which either can deter problem behavior or make it easier. The focus mainly is on the small and middle size libraries which do not have security forces of their own, and which constitute the majority of all public libraries in the nation. Although

much of the specific advice comes from the security professionals, I
have tried to collect guidelines, procedures, and ideas which can be
implemented by library staffs working only with their local police
forces.

With regard to physical arrangements, there are many of us
around the country saddled with inappropriate buildings—or those
ironies of modern design—the prize-winning structure that looks so
wonderful in the four color spreads of *Architectural Record*, but turns
out to be a security nightmare to work in. Even in the worst buildings,
however, there are some ameliorative steps that can be taken. And on
this score, the local police can often be helpful.

Working with the Police

Librarians want two things from the police: trust that when library
staff calls, the cops will believe them, and quick response time.
Achieving those objectives requires building a collegial relationship in
which both the library staff and the police understand each other's
work environment. It was suggested in Chapter 5 that this means
bridging the gap between library staff values and those of the police.

One way to do this is for the library director to ask the chief of
police to assist in conducting a security assessment of the library
building. Even if the library is not able (or is unwilling) to take all the
advice given, at least the police officers will develop some understanding of how the library works and why it does what it does.

It is also remarkable what cops can think up if they are invited to
be part of the prevention process, rather than merely the cleaner-up-
pers at the end.

For example, a few years ago we were having trouble with
"sleepovers" at the downtown branch of the Santa Cruz library. Street
people (we assumed) would elude the security sweep conducted by the
staff at closing time, and spend the night in the building. We didn't
have enough money to hire a night guard, and the Police Department
was stretched too thin to provide more than semiregular checkups of
the building exterior.

One day, genius struck our police chief.

"Listen," he said on the phone. "You can help me solve a problem,
and I think I've got a solution for you, too. I've got these canine units?
Well, they have to be trained all the time. How would you feel about

my cops using the library as a training site? We'd bring in the dogs and their officers, say, three nights a week, and do an exercise with them in your building. What time does your computer operator come on?"

"About five a.m.," I said.

"Perfect," said the chief. "We'd be in and out between midnight and four a.m. We've got warning decals you could put on the doors. What do you think?"

"Perfect," I said. And we have never had another sleepover problem. When the computer operator changed her hours, she got introduced to the canine units, and they are all the best of friends. She says the dogs are very sweet when they know you. You can even pet them.

Security Surveys, Part I: Buildings

Every security expert, management consultant, and police officer advises that librarians make security surveys of their building and operations. The survey needs to look at the building in terms of how potential problem behaviors (flashing, purse snatching, vandalism and the like) are made easier by the physical arrangement. A library also needs to assess what its current problem behaviors are, and consider how physical changes and modifications in operations would help.

Stack Areas

Stacks are the great security bane of all libraries. It is a pity we need them to shelve the books, because they offer so much potential for criminal use. They are tall for easy hiding behind, fixed in place so that they can't be moved without major money and effort, there are long aisles between them which require exits at both ends, and their lighting must run the same way they do if the contents of the shelves is to be seen. This latter point is particularly annoying, because it reduces flexibility in solving security problems: one starts out to turn the stacks to run at a better angle for sight lines from the Circulation Desk, only to realize that every single ceiling fixture will also have to be moved. That will be another $2,000 please.

A favorite ploy of architects, and a real temptation for librarians too, is to use the wall-like stacks to create nifty little nooks and crannies in which to shelve the odd subject collection (genealogy, historic cookbooks, and the like). But these can create terrible security problems. If special small areas cannot be seen by the staff, and aren't well lit, they can easily become havens for, even invitations to, problem behavior.

Many small and midsized libraries are arranged so that the stacks radiate out from a central area. Space is preserved at the far ends for access, and the end passage is often left wide enough for study carrels or tables. This is not a good idea. All sitting/reading/study space in a library should have good sight lines to the exit doors for their users and be reasonably easy to see by staff. Even though it makes for a noisier environment, it is best to keep the tables and other sitting areas out in the main area if at all possible.

Restrooms

These are another bane, and again, it is a great pity that libraries are public facilities, and therefore need (and are often required) to offer restrooms to users. Restroom security problems are a little easier to reduce than those of bookstacks, however. The object is to ensure that the facilities are available for secure, unharassed use by those who need them.

One relatively inexpensive option is to install devices which keep the restroom lights on at all times. With such a system, lights must be turned off at a master control, thereby preventing (for instance) a man with criminal intent from reaching around the women's room door, flicking off the lights, and coming in. Or a jokey kid doing the same thing. This kind of device can be installed in any library area—a back hall, the lobby leading to the meeting room, that cul-de-sac which no one knows why was in the design plan—where guaranteed lighting would be a good idea.

Security consultants sometimes also recommend installing emergency telephones in restrooms and other isolated areas. This sounds like asking for trouble to me, but a library might investigate it if it has the money (lots) and thinks it would solve a local problem.

Restrooms located away from the beaten path—down a long hall or in the basement—can be a nightmare. Even if locked, protecting children going to and from them is very hard. The best solution is to move them. If that can't be done, then try installing hallway-reflecting mirrors, to keep some tabs on what is going on. Another solution is video surveillance, or even *fake* video surveillance. Apparently it is not difficult to purchase or rig up the kind of cameras which look like they are photographing activities in a certain area, when in fact they are not. Of course, standard sensibilities require that these cameras not be in positions to intrude on users' private activities, so this is not a panacea. But the police department can give you advice on a security firm which handles this kind of equipment.

The best way to promote restroom security is to keep the facilities locked. This is an option that the desk staff may hate, since it creates key-handing-out and time-monitoring work for them, and some of the public won't like it much either. On the other hand, it is one of the only ways to prevent misuse and abuse of restrooms. Explained in these terms, the staff and public alike have a basis for understanding and agreement. Separate restrooms for children, limited exclusively to their use, and again controlled by keys, offer the best restroom security protection against child molesters. Locking the restrooms also helps cut down on the pilfering of toilet paper and paper towels, because the staff can require that totes, backpacks, etc. — if allowed in the first place (and perhaps they shouldn't be) — be left at the desk in exchange for the key.

Finally, if the library building is an old one, or is located in a shopping center or other nontraditional space, check all the doors, and especially those to the restrooms. Are the key slots of the locks on the correct side? Is there a button lock on the inside of a door where you don't want one (for example, the children's restroom)? Before you laugh, think how infuriated (and frightened) you would be if you got locked in a hallway which you couldn't exit. This happened at the Boston Public Library a few years ago, and the trapped woman died.

Library Entrances and Exits

Adequate lighting is the usual security issue here. A conscientious librarian will walk in and out of the building at night, experimenting with various routes to the bus stop, the parking lot, or a major cross street. Is there enough ambient light so that a user of any age feels comfortable walking to a parked car? Is there also adequate light on the disabled access ramp? Can the sidewalk be seen well enough to ensure that most patrons won't trip on hazards such as broken concrete?

Every library, no matter how small, needs at least two entrances, so that the building can be evacuated safely in case of fire or earthquake. The second entrance can have an alarm device on it to ensure that it is only used in emergencies. The locksmith can be asked to put a fifteen or twenty second time delay on the lock. This will help the staff get there in time to catch a thief stealing books (or at least see which way the thief is heading).

Staff entrances present an additional group of problems. First there is the great tendency to leave them unlocked. This is especially true if not every staff person (or volunteer) has a key. If only library personnel used the back door, this wouldn't be a problem. But every delivery person, citizen wanting to donate books, patron off the street looking for a short cut, and the odd wallet thief, also wants to use the staff entrance. Keep it locked. Insist that the staff and other legitimate users ring the bell if they don't have a key.

Another reason why staff entrance security is important is because so many of these doors are located at the back of the technical services area. This gives any unsupervised delivery person, not to mention that woman the staff thought was a volunteer but doesn't seem to be around anymore, easy access to a very precious commodity: the books, CDs, cassettes, and videos lined up on the shelves waiting for processing. Naked of any property markings, they are ripe for the picking by a quick-fingered thief.

Security experts advise, by the way, that libraries look carefully at their processing procedures: get new items into the pipeline as fast as possible, with property stamping an early step. This doesn't necessarily cut down on pilfering for personal use, but it does help prevent organized conspiracies to steal from the library and resell to used book stores or on the streets. Another good idea is to move the shelves where the just-unpacked books are kept out of the main traffic stream.

Microform Machines, OPACs and Other Equipment

The security issue here is vandalism. Microfilm machines and public access catalog terminals need to be located in places where they are visible to the staff. And if that cannot be done in all cases, at least put them in places where other members of the public can see them. Most people are willing to report abuse when they see it, even if they don't find themselves able to intervene personally.

Keys and Name Tags

Theoretically, only staff (never volunteers, trustees, or members of the Library Friends group) should have exterior keys to the building. This is a hard rule to enforce, however, if only for convenience reasons. Who on a small staff really wants to be the one to get out of bed on Sunday morning and truck down to the library to let in the Friends president, who left something behind when she was here yesterday for the book sale.

If tight control of who gets keys cannot be enforced, at least organize the key program carefully. Make sure that the bare minimum of people have master keys which open every lock. The rest should get separate keys for each space. Never issue a key without writing it down on a master list, and do the same when one is loaned. Make getting keys back a check off item when an employee leaves, and make turning in keys a condition of getting the final paycheck. If payroll checks are issued from a separate city office, this will require coordination, but that should not be hard: finance people are notably security conscious.

Maybe if we called name tags "security tags" there wouldn't be such fuss from staff about wearing them. The point of a tag is to identify who is an employee or person with a valid reason for being in the staff areas of the library, and who isn't. If only ten people work in the building, security tags aren't necessary because everyone knows everyone else.

Even small libraries, however, may have a constantly changing group of student pages, who turn up for work at odd hours looking like typical high school or college kids. It is impossible for anyone but their supervisor to keep track of who they are. Require them to wear buttons which say *Library Page*. Get comparable buttons for volunteers and Friends of the Library.

Using buttons (which are cheap) is also good public relations: it identifies people on the floor who might be able to answer a directional question, and it advertises the volunteer program and the Friends organization.

As for staff security tags, the principal objection to them seems to be that displaying the employee's first and last name is a security violation in itself. Oh, come. The name part of a permanent tag can go on the back side. The point is to identify who is a legitimate staffer at the library.

Signage

Security experts set great store by having readable, well-lit signs. There are two reasons. The first is that fire and other regulations require that exits on every floor be clearly identified. The second is the overall ambience of the library: if the directional and location signs are accurate and make sense, the image of an orderly institution in which appropriate behavior is expected is enhanced.

Frank DeRosa, the director of Facilities Management and Risk Control at the Brooklyn Public Library (and the man who told the ALA audience about the usefulness of wet thread) is also a strong advocate of posted rules signs. He says a common response from a library user who is asked to stop doing something is, "Show me where it sez. . ." (Or in California, "Hey, man, like, show me where it says. . ."). Pointing out the sign which says no smoking or whatever is a good response. On the second request to cease and desist, the Brooklyn Public Library security staff give the perpetrator a five-by-seven inch handbill which lists the behavior rules. This sounds like a good idea for any size library.

Security Surveys, Part II: Assessing Current Problems

The second part of a security survey of the library is a look at current problems. What are the typical broken rules, criminal acts, or behaviors the library is experiencing. A rash of flasher incidents? A series of stolen wallet reports? As one security expert put it, assessing security problems is largely a matter of asking the right questions. The old journalism mnemonic is useful here: Look for the five W's: Who, What, When, Where, and Why, although not necessarily in that order. And the answers to these questions should provide clues for how operations or furniture arrangements or whatever might be adjusted.

For example, if theft of patron possessions is a mounting problem, perhaps the library should think about increasing the number of "Don't leave your backpack or purse unattended" signs. Or taping small cards with the same message to every table and study carrel. If the library believes that men are hanging about in the children's room for unacceptable reasons, it should look at taking out the lounge chairs, even if this makes it more difficult for parents to read comfortably to their children. Are many of the problems occurring at one time period each day (for instance, just after school dismisses, or in the period before the soup kitchen opens)? What about deploying as many pages as possible during those hours, so there is a big staff presence on the floor?

Hearsay and anecdotal descriptions at staff meetings are not enough to determine what a library's security problems are. Documentation is needed, and to document such things a library needs a form. Even the staff at a tiny one-room facility in the middle of the desert needs to write down, clearly and coherently, what happened when that green convertible screeched to a halt in front of the building, and Thelma and Louise jumped out and rushed through the door, making off with the week's accumulated overdue fine money. Actually, it was only $5.35, so they won't get far, but still...

Seriously: Appendix F includes a sample Incident Report Form. Staff should be trained to use these whenever anything out of the ordinary occurs. Among other reasons, the forms are a means for laying a good paper trail. And the library will need one if it decides to secure a no trespassing order against a patron. Branch managers will find that the forms are a useful way of keeping central administration aware of how tough things are on the front lines, and the administration can use them to document emerging problems and budget requests.

Planning a New Building

All of the rules regarding security evaluations in an existing building should be adapted in planning a new one. The magic of a new facility is that—potentially at least—the library gets to start from scratch, with shelving lined up the right way, adequate lighting, restrooms in visible places, windows in the doors of offices so they can be easily inspected, and even a staff entrance separate from the technical services department.

Actually, it is sometimes very difficult to get these kinds of security protections built into the plans for a new building, especially working with an architect who hasn't designed a library before. Many are the award winning buildings which have impossible sight lines and are filled with obscure corners. It is therefore always smart to get a library building consultant on the project who will look out for the library's security and other interests as the plans and specifications are evaluated. Sad to say, the advice of such a consultant carries more weight than the requests of a working librarian who is saying the same thing, even when what's being asked for is just good common sense (a circulation desk near the front entrance, stairwells which can be inspected easily, regular shapes, and so forth).

Ten Minutes a Week for Training

It is astonishing how difficult it is to get staff, particularly those at the busiest sites, to remember to fill out Incident Reports. Actually, the problem isn't getting them to remember to do it, it is getting them to take the time to do it. To reinforce the consciousness of necessity, a library might devote an occasional training session to a discussion of the form and when and how it is filled out.

Another useful training discussion topic is a review of the month's incidents and how they were handled: this is always good for morale if they were handled well, and teaches a good deal even if they weren't. Ask questions of the people who confront the problems: would moving the furniture fix it? Does the library need a daily walk-through from the police? Suppose we simply closed that restroom off, and made everyone use the facility on the main floor?

The principal sources of this chapter were: American Library Association, LAMA Buildings and Equipment Section Committee on Safety and Security in Library Buildings, "Is Your Library an Accessory to Crime?" Program at Annual Conference, June 29, 1992, cassette tapes; and DeRosa, Frank J., director, Facilities Management and Risk Control, Brooklyn Public Library, telephone interview, November 9, 1992.

9. *Writing Good Manuals*

It occurs to me that there are only two kinds of library staff manuals—the kind people read or use, and the kind they don't. As it happens, I have ample experience with both, and I can tell you there are few things more satisfying than seeing a manual you've spent days and weeks putting together actually being used, and used effectively. On the other hand, how humiliating it is to find one's brilliantly conceived instructional handbook gathering dust on a hidden shelf under the reference desk!

The Santa Cruz Library staff and I spent much of the summer of 1988 putting together comprehensive emergency manuals for each of our library branches.

In October, 1989, disaster struck: a major earthquake wreaked substantial havoc throughout this section of California. We had roughly 350,000 books spilled onto the floor systemwide, and other major damage, but every branch was evacuated safely, and we opened for service again only six days later. Staff had read the manual and knew what to do. They had inventoried all emergency supplies two weeks before the earthquake, right on the manual's schedule. This meant that every flashlight was where it was supposed to be, and even had a working battery.

On the other hand, I was the lead author of an automation system manual which met a primary need during the first year or so we were on line, but increasingly became less useful. Either the manual was too simple for a staff which became very automation-savvy quite quickly, or the system was too complicated for the kind of information the manual endeavored to convey. Probably it was both. A staff committee wrote the successor manual, which is twice the length of the original— and in several places, well over my head with details that only primary users of the system would know. All the circulation staff people think the new version is just great. "You can *find* things in it," they report happily. I try not to be hurt by the implications of this comment.

These two examples lead me to draw some conclusions about what constitutes a good staff manual. The first is that one must be very clear about the purpose such a document is meant to serve, and then design and write it to meet that objective.

An emergency manual, for example, is supposed to tell the staff exactly what to do when an earthquake hits ("Duck, Cover, and Hold," as we say in California), or how long to keep the library open if the power goes off. The whole point is to give precise information and instructions. What is wanted is a document which can be referred to quickly in, dare I say it, an emergency. Explanations are nice, but not required. And in fact, explication of the whys and wherefores of rabies vaccination can get in the way of the hard information about what to do if a dog bites a patron.

An automation system manual, on the other hand, has a lot more room for explanation, because its primary purpose is as a training and reference tool—staff check it when they can't remember how to do something.

Some manuals are giant compendiums of all the information the library staff has about its internal operations. Santa Cruz has one like that—it is called the Public Services Manual, and it contains policies, procedures, and explanations on everything from the method for distributing paychecks to the annual branch weeding schedule. Kept in one of those giant three ring binders, it weighs in at eleven and a quarter pounds. I sometimes think its real purpose is to allow management staff to say to errant branch workers, "How could you not have known that? The procedure is right there in the Public Services Manual. Oh? You haven't looked at your manual lately? Tsk, tsk."

It must be obvious that I don't think much of the style, the content, or the basic idea of the Public Services Manual, but the last time I tried to substitute something else, the branch managers went through the ceiling. They like it because it consolidates in one place everything they ever wanted to know about what the Central Office has thought up to torment them: annual property inventories, monthly reports, and the like.

Another manual-writing criterion is the intended audience. Obviously, there is a vast difference between what we write about the automation system for the people who must operate it, e.g., the circulation and technical services staff, and what we might put in a training manual for the pages, who don't work the circulation desk, but may be called on to help a confused user at a public access catalog terminal.

There is also a difference in style if we are writing for training, or writing for reference, or writing for both. And this point brings me to the issue of what might constitute a useful manual to help staff handle problem situations in libraries.

Problem Situation Manuals — Purpose, Style, and Content

In the course of working on this book I have collected several examples of staff problem situation (or "problem patron" or "customer relations") manuals. They seem to fall into two genres: the ones with short and precise instructions for what to do about a specific problem, and those which are longer because they feature more explanation and narrative.

I have also observed that the concise ones have a certain similarity, leading me to believe that either there is a central computer somewhere into which each staff committee assigned to write a manual is secretly plugged, or, the same tattered copy of the Original Problem Patron Manual is being passed from library to library.

Back in 1984, when the Santa Cruz Library staff prepared its first manual (called *Problem Patrons: A Coping Manual for Staff*) we cribbed most of it from a comparable document prepared by the Schenectady County (New York) Public Library. Seven years later the hot new manual being described in the press was from a library in Southern California. The new lingo was "customer" rather than "patron," but most of the procedures were straight from Schenectady. And when I wrote to a library director in Texas for permission to use a section of her library's manual in Appendix F, she very nicely wrote back to say that in fact the procedure I was interested in had been taken from a manual produced by a library in the Northwest, and perhaps I should go directly to the source. It turned out theirs was based on Schenectady too.

Clearly, one thing which governs the style of a manual is the experience of the staff. In reviewing the record, I note with some surprise that back in 1984 the Santa Cruz staff committee and I were at pains to provide careful and usually colorless instructions on how to handle things such as "Suspicious Behavior" and "Assault." The Appendix was larded with quotations from the state penal code and instructions and diagrams for self-defense, such as

> Strike, kick, stomp, jab, or poke these vulnerable parts as fast and as hard as you can. If your target is the nose, do not just hit the nose, aim through the nose to the back of the head.

It occurs to me that this was a response provoked by a staff confronting a time of great change: increasing numbers of street people were appearing in the library, many workers were worried for their personal safety, new user groups were making demands for service, the library was in the process of automating, and to top it all off, a new director had come to town.

So the staff committee wrote a manual which included a procedure for every conceivable eventuality. These days I wonder if we might have handled the situation better by doing a lot of talking at small staff meetings, in order to inject a little more reality into the common consciousness. I mean, after all—punching "through the nose to the back of the head"? Wonder women? Bruce Lee at the Circ Desk? Mercifully, this is a section that never had to be applied. On the other hand, the resulting manual was regarded as a boon by everyone.

Our current problem situation manual (it appears as Appendix F) is a good deal more relaxed in its approach. It reflects revised assumptions about what our task is, our rights as a library staff to protect ourselves and our patrons, and our knowledge that our worst and most frequent problems are going to be with angry people, not with sexual deviants or street people. We certainly contend with problems created by the latter categories, but I think the staff now has an easy confidence (based on experience and training) in its ability to handle them.

I don't know whether the transition from precise procedures to a narrative approach is evolutionary, but I do believe that the third edition of our manual (now called *Handling Problem Situations in the Library—A Training and Reference Manual for Staff*) is a good deal more interesting to read than the 1984 document. I have included it as an Appendix because it illustrates most of my prejudices and convictions about manual writing.

Purpose of Problem Situation Manuals

A good problem situation manual has one basic purpose: to tell staff what to do, and how to do it, when a problem comes up. It should reflect the policies and procedures upon which the staff is supposed to base its actions. That is, it should answer basic questions, such as who calls the police when an incident occurs: the staff person on the line, or a supervisor.

And it should also convey, in its basic style, how we want the staff to interact with the public. If we expect the staff to be formal, cold, and rigid in their approach, then by all means write a manual which is colorless, tight-lipped, dry, and sniffy. If we are striving for interactions with the public which are relaxed and friendly, then try to use manual language which is warmer.

A useful manual should not be a document which we thrust into the hands of a new staff person, saying, "Oh, yes, and read this by Monday—it's got a lot of good stuff you need to know." The manual has to be the basis for training of two sorts: what is provided to newcomers, and on-going discussions at staff meetings. Chapter 10 discusses training more thoroughly.

Good manuals also are organic documents. They grow and change. Sometimes they get thrown out altogether and something better substituted (see the Santa Cruz automation manual experience). One of the most important things that can come out of training discussions at regular staff meetings is information about what needs to be added or changed in the existing manual. Reviewing incident reports has the same purpose. Someone on the library's management staff should take responsibility for ensuring that the problem situation manual is kept up to date—that it addresses new problems as they arise, takes cognizance of new laws as they are passed, and is periodically freshened up with new examples or at least a new cover.

Finally, a problem situation manual has to take account of the different situations of different branches. The resources upon which a downtown branch can rely (three minute response time from the police, for example) are vastly different than those of more isolated facilities.

While the basic policies must be the same, a good manual will include variable procedures which take cognizance of small branches as well as medium-size and large.

Notes on Style

Whether of the Concise genre or the Narrative, manuals should be written in the second person singular or plural, and in the active, rather than passive voice. If you mean that you want a staff person to behave or to do something in a certain way, say so directly. It is better to write,

> *Tell the patron, "No, you may not do . . ."*
> than
> *Patrons should be told that they may not . . .*

Use definite language. Avoid waffling words such as "seems," or "perhaps," or "possibly," unless of course these words are appropriate to the context. Put the topic at the beginning of the sentence, and try to keep sentences short. Do not confuse the words "may" and "can." The former means "allow" and the latter "able," as "Videos may be checked out for two days only," versus "You can check out videos at the library."

Give staff precise language to use in as many situations as you possibly can. It is not that the staff will necessarily use the language you provide—they are not automatons, after all, and we are not interested in creating a corps of robots. But having language filed away in one's head for what to say to a person who has just set off the security system alarm ("Excuse me, but I think we forgot to check out your library materials") can be very helpful to a staff person who has just been surprised by a ringing bell while coping with a line of people waiting for service.

Writing sample language can be a useful technique for training, too. Asking a staff group to discuss a particular problem, and to come up with the best language to use in handling it, is a good way to help everyone clarify the nature of the problem, remind themselves of the library's procedure for handling it, and find words which people are comfortable using.

Content

It is very easy, when creating a problem situation manual, to get bored about two-thirds of the way through the process (or sooner), and start eliminating ideas for the contents. "Oh surely we don't need that level of detail," someone will argue, and out will go the information on what to do when a patron tries to get past the circulation desk with a book from which he or she has torn the barcode label.

Actually, however, the more the examples and discussions of problems there are, the better. One reason is that it is reassuring to staff who might otherwise believe that they are the only ones in the whole world who ever received an obscene phone call, or got taken to the cleaners (verbally) by an irate patron. Another reason is that people almost always respond better when they are not surprised by events. Being prepared for the unexpected in patron behavior makes for a calm response. Finally, an encyclopedic manual (or at least one which tries to cover most of the categories of problem situations staff encounter) is a good way to remind trainers of what they must cover during the orientation of new employees.

The Manual Writing Process

A very common method for getting a problem situation manual (or any other kind) written is for a staff committee to take on the job. There are good reasons for this. Probably the best one is that it involves the people on the front line, who after all have the most experience in handling problem situations, in writing up the response procedures. Provided the staff understand the library's basic philosophy and policies, the procedures they produce are likely to be far more useful than something management thinks up in a back room.

Asking a staff committee to write the manual also creates a corps of people who can serve as trainers when the manual is introduced to the rest of the staff. Moreover, they will be advocates for those procedures and methods which other staff find difficult to believe will actually work.

The trouble with a staff manual writing committee is that the process takes so long. This is especially true if the committee decides to be original, instead of adapting another library's manual to local conditions. And of course, documents developed by committee have a terrible tendency to read as though a camel actually did write them.

Here's an ideal scenario for a manual writing process. It tries to use the expertise of staff at the same time that it hurries the process along.

1. Somebody, probably the person (the director?) who decided

the staff needed a manual, should collect some examples of typical problem situation manuals from other libraries. The samples in Appendix F suggest some places to write, and the whole Santa Cruz manual is there too. Any library is free to copy it (with appropriate credit, of course).

2. A small committee of staff, led by a senior manager, but including a floor supervisor or someone from the public service desks, should be appointed. If your library is a multibranch system, find a way to include a staff person from one of the smaller branches, who can speak to the issue of what works when you are on your own. The committee's first task is to review the manuals, decide on a format (concise or narrative), and agree on whether the sample manuals from other libraries can be adapted to local needs. Based on this decision, the committee should develop a time schedule for completing a draft manual.

3. Assuming an adaptation of an existing manual, the committee should decide on the contents. What problem situations does this library need to be sure to cover?

4. Then, it should review each section of the model to be used, and identify the problem situation areas for which the library lacks policy. These should be taken to the director and management staff for guidance, plus a reminder of what the production schedule for the manual is.

5. While management staff works on needed policies, the manual committee can work on revising the sample manual's procedures to fit the local situation. The senior manager should assign sections to each person, so that the committee doesn't start talking as a group about a procedure until it has a first draft with which to work.

Here's where consultation with line staff is absolutely crucial. If a committee member is assigned the section on handling a rowdy drunk, for instance, or someone spaced out on drugs, that person should interview desk workers who last dealt with such a problem. What did they say? How did they get the person out the door? Did their actions match library policy? Try the sample manual's procedures on the desk workers, and see whether they think they are a fair rendition of what should be done.

The next step is to write a draft, and take it back to the people on the line. Revisions should be based on their comments. It is certainly possible that staff informants are not going to have creative ideas for words to use in a difficult situation, or other suggestions. If this is the case, the committee will need to think up the proper language for what to say or do.

6. The committee will probably also want to consult with the local police department for advice on techniques and procedures.

7. The director and others also should be consulting with staff as they work on developing the missing policies upon which procedures are based. Frequently, by the time a policy has been negotiated, the procedures for implementing it are obvious. But be careful here. It is a trap to think that writing up a good statement of the library's policy is the same as thinking through and writing out careful procedures for implementing it. The manual, after all, is aimed at all workers, from the youngest and least sophisticated page to senior reference staff.

8. The completed first draft probably needs to be reviewed by the director and whatever other senior managers exist. A meeting to discuss revisions is frequently helpful. It gives the director an opportunity to say directly why she or he doesn't like a procedure being proposed, and the committee a chance to argue back in favor of methods the staff feels strongly about.

9. The next stop might be the office of the jurisdiction's legal counsel. The director should initiate this, and be prepared to argue for flexibility and for the library's mission.

10. After a clean-up revision based on these reviews, send the manual out to various of the library's key departments or supervisors. Be sure to include branches of various sizes. Set deadlines for response, and if it looks like there is going to be a lot of trouble (as, "Well, I'm sorry, but that is *not* the way we do it at the Mostly Branch"), get everyone together for a "Let's trash the draft manual" session. Think of it as the first round in the training process.

11. All these drafts will have revealed some of the formatting options provided by your word processing equipment or creative staff typists. The object is to make the manual easy to read and use (or accessible, as we say in the library business), as well as attractive. Strive for openness, clarity of organization, and lots of white space.

Three ring binders are a frequent cover choice, because they make updating simple. On the other hand, if you guess that you are going to need a new edition every year anyway, and really want to be able to give every single staff person his or her own copy, it might be less expensive to stick with comb binding or staples.

12. With a final document in hand, discuss how to introduce it to all staff, training them on its contents and use. See the next chapter for some suggestions on how to do this, and particularly for the role of the hardworking manual committee, which in my ideal scenario, does not get to disband for another twelve months at least. And boy, do they love that. Committees groan like camels, too.

10. Training Staff

A friend of mine who is a former employee of a very large bank once described to me the on-going training program her bank offered to the tellers and other people on the front lines. I had asked about this because I thought bank people must need to learn about how to handle customers who are mad or otherwise difficult, and I wanted to know how the pros in the private sector did it. How did management teach bank staff to deal with people who are angry at declining interest rates, a rejected loan application, or simply a long wait in line at the teller windows?

"Well," said my friend, "of course you realize the primary purpose of training at the bank was to integrate people into the corporate culture. They had a few courses in DOS when computers were first coming in, and so forth. But a lot of it was that so-called 'personal growth' stuff, like Dress for Success and Learn Your Colors. We were expected to take those, by the way, whether we needed to or not. Did you know I am definitely 'winter'? And since we were in a bank, of course there were seminars on Managing Your Money and Planning Your Retirement."

"What about communication skills, and dealing with the public?" I asked.

"Oh, they didn't bother with that much," she said. "I guess they didn't think it was a real need. We did have the people's money already, after all."

So much for learning from the private sector. However, at least one important point came up in this conversation: the role of training in integrating people into the culture of the organization.

My friend's view of her bank's "organizational culture" was somewhat disparaging, which is why she no longer works there. She believed the bank principally valued employees who thought the same

119

and looked the same, and that the "human resources development" people responsible for the training program were working to ensure that as many employees as possible achieved that objective.

While I share her distaste for training programs aimed at turning out Ken and Barbie dolls for the public service desks, I do think it is fair to acknowledge that when librarians talk about training staff at least one of our objectives is inculcating workers with the library's organizational culture or style. That applies whether the focus of the training is problem situations or just everyday interaction with the public. We work hard to hire people who seem as though they have what it takes to succeed on the front desk. But then our obligation is to give them the information and skills they need to do the work, and do it in a way that matches our conception of the kind of place our public library is supposed to be.

That conception will not be the same for all public libraries, nor indeed for all the branches within a single library system. Service at a tiny neighborhood branch, where the staff is likely to know the names of most of the regulars *and* their grandchildren, is different from the style at the downtown library, where there is almost always a line of two or three people waiting for help at the reference desk. Basic style for interacting with the public is modified by the circumstances of daily reality. Nevertheless, conveying what the library is after in its relations with patrons, whatever that may be, is a basic objective of training.

Underneath the somewhat loosely and variably defined umbrella of "style," however, there are three basic objectives that any effective problem situation training program will feature: ensuring that staff knows and understands library policies and procedures, teaching appropriate skills for implementing those policies and procedures, and providing a means for on-going discussion and communication about problem situations.

The literature of education reminds us of two very important points. The first is the distinction between education and training.[1] Education is what we learn for the long term. It is useful whether one's job changes or not. Among other things, it enables us to analyze and extrapolate even as conditions change. Training, on the other hand, teaches skills for a particular time and place. The payoff is immediate.

The other important point is that adults learn best when the learning is based on their experience.[2] You can lecture at them all you like, but if you really want them to get the message, you have to put the material in the context of what they already know. If they don't have relevant experience, then it is wise to find a technique, such as role playing, which gives them experience on the spot.

Training New Workers

My definition of heaven is a place where every writer of letters to the editor of the local newspaper who proposes that the public library can be run with volunteers has to take the initial training we give to each library clerk who joins our regular staff. If the letter writers don't fall apart over automation system procedures for handling requests, they will certainly flunk when they get to skills for telling a patron that they can't check out any more videos until they pay off the $9.99 they owe in back fines.

Most libraries, even the smallest and poorest, invest an incredible number of hours in teaching new staff the technical basics of their work, whether it is circulation desk procedures or reference clerical support. Many of them attempt to dedicate training time to personal communication skills, as well, and to procedures for handling problems created by difficult patron behavior.

I think it is fair to say, however, that as our automation systems grow more complex, and the number of services staff can provide to the public increases, more time must be spent on technical training. Skill in handling problem situations is increasingly left to on-the-job mentoring by supervisors.

One way to compensate is to have a good problem situation manual, which can be used to back up a minimal training session (say an hour?) on "how we handle problem situations at this library." Giving a lengthy manual to a new staff person to read is one way of saying, "This is what happens here; this is how we try to do things."

It can also be a means, alas, for scaring the daylights out of the newcomer. The less sophisticated ones will not let too much time pass before they whisper to a new colleague, "Are they kidding? Does stuff like this really go on here?" Yes, is the answer, it does, and the sooner new workers understand that, the sooner they will be competent on the public desks. I once heard a library director remark that one of the purposes of new staff training is to let them know that public libraries are *not* necessarily pleasant places in which to work.

At any rate, the frequent outcome of the pressure to teach as much as we can in a short time is that we send new people to the public desks with only sketchy training in problem situation handling, but a reasonably thorough understanding of the worst they can expect from the library users. It is therefore very important to make sure that the workers' supervisors take responsibility for completing the training process. The first part of this needs to be a reality check ("No, dear, the majority of our patrons are very nice people, really"). And there probably should be a checklist of discussions and experiences for the worker.

One on-the-job training device is to partner the new worker with someone more experienced. Indeed, it is a good idea to appoint an official mentor for every new person who joins the staff. The mentor's job is to give the newcomer the inside scoop on all the things missed in training (why the soft drink machine only takes quarters) and to be responsible for showing her or him the real score, as opposed to the theoretical one taught in training.

The other important mentoring task is to make sure the novice gets a chance to observe a more senior staff member handling (for example) an angry patron—and talk about it afterwards. Was "stand and deliver" necessary in this case, or did paraphrasing work? Is the worker satisfied with the outcome of the encounter, or does she feel in retrospect that she could have done better? This kind of debriefing exercise makes all workers conscious of how they are handling stressful encounters, and establishes the pattern of communication among co-workers which is crucial to effective management of difficult situations.

Most organizations have performance appraisal processes built into their personnel regulations, sometimes including three month and six month probationary evaluations. Unfortunately, the appraisals are all too frequently based on standardized municipal forms, meant to be used for all classes of employees, from trash collectors to library clerks. This makes it difficult for a line supervisor to use appraisal as a tool for improving individual employee performance. At the very least, however, the appraisal interview can be a time for talking with a new worker about problem situation experiences, and providing some advice and instruction. The performance objectives which ought to be part of the appraisal can include things such as rereading and thinking about a section of the manual, ordinary observation, or practicing a particular skill with another worker.

Finally, of course, it is important to give new workers off-desk time to do the manual reading and one-on-one practice with other staff which is necessary for training. No one would deny how difficult this can be in a busy library, but it is important.

On-going Staff Training

At a recent state library conference I entertained myself by asking my colleagues how much time they put into on-going staff training in handling problem situations. Although several cited day-long staff workshops (organized by their own libraries or by a regional consortium), the majority response was eyes raised to heaven.

"I know, I know," said one. "We should be keeping people's skills sharp on this. And problems are getting more frequent, too. We have a manual, and I know people are using it. But honestly! There just doesn't seem to be time for more than that."

I followed up by asking whether building a short period of problem situation training into every staff meeting would be a useful device. Most thought it might be, but they were not entirely sure how the line supervisors would take to it. Staff meeting time is short too, with heavy agendas built into tiny windows of time between getting the bookdrop cleared and opening for the day.

In Chapter 3 I suggested the "Ten Minutes a Week for Training" model because I am convinced that frequent talk about problem situations is a crucial method of helping staff deal with them effectively.

Sharing the experience of long term staff and relieving stress by the therapy of talking are only two of the more obvious reasons. I also suggested that a good staff discussion of a bad situation provides management with invaluable insight into what is actually happening on the library floor.

An underlying theme of the present book has been that effective handling of problem situations depends upon open communication among workers. People in one department or branch must have opportunities to tell each other when curious or difficult incidents take place, if only to provide alerts as to what may be coming down next. This is not simply passing around Polaroid pictures of known flashers, so everyone can be alert to the potential problem. It is also sharing information so that collective solutions can be found.

The branch manager who has never had to deal with a highly

verbal, mentally ill street person can be coached through the trauma by staff who have — if they know it is happening to the branch manager. But unless mechanisms for public (e.g., staff meeting) discussion of problem situations are built into on-going library life, this might not happen. Of course the afflicted branch manager will talk about it to her staff friends, but "whine" about it at an open staff meeting? Forget it, unless talk is part of the normal operating mode.

The major problem with the Ten Minutes a Week for Training idea is limiting it to ten minutes. I am pretty sure, however, that if supervisors find themselves with a problem situation discussion which staff are unwilling to terminate, then the technique has done what it is supposed to: opened a window on a problem which people need to talk about. I also think that as problem situation discussions become routine, it will be easier for staff to limit their talking time.

Each of the preceding problem situation chapters provided discussion questions or incidents for staff meeting use. A staff getting into the spirit of the thing will have little trouble thinking up variations which reflect local conditions. And the suggestions are not meant to substitute for a report and discussion of an actual incident and how the staff involved handled it.

Many libraries are lucky enough to have a senior manager who is responsible for staff training — coordinating who gets to go where to learn what, and how new hires are taken through the standard training process.

In smaller operations, this is one of the many balls which the library director must juggle. In either case, it is a good idea to have an on-going annual training plan. The plan helps keep track of when the staff last discussed handling sexual deviancy cases, for instance, or how many months it has been since everyone was "refreshed" on the procedures for responding to book complaints. Given that there are other training issues to be worked into the standard calendar (periodic reviews of emergency procedures, for example), it becomes very important to systematize this process.

Workshops as a Training Technique

Organizing a half-day or an all-day workshop for training is a popular way to get the job done, and has many advantages. For one thing, attending the workshop gets people out of the library, or at least off the public desks. And when the workshop brings staff from several libraries together, it can be especially interesting.

On the other hand, a workshop organized by a regional consortium limits the number of people who can attend, so it can't be relied upon as the primary training tool. The best that one can hope for is that staff who attend will bring the information home and share it with those left behind.

Several good books have been written about organizing workshops, among them Ruth Warncke's *Planning Library Workshops and Institutes* and *Preparing, Designing, and Leading Workshops* by Susan Cooper and Cathy Heenan.[3] One of the basic points these authors make is that it is crucial to be very clear about both the purpose and the audience for the workshop.

A half-day regional workshop called something like "Handling Problem Situations in the Library" is, to my mind, doomed to failure. The topic is far too broad. Most participants will go away with an expanded knowledge of the infinite and varied problems library staffs face, but not many new skills in how to handle them.

On the other hand, a workshop which aims to improve the skills of people in handling angry or irate patrons offers a chance of real learning. It can be organized to focus on teaching two or three skills (active listening, for example), with plenty of time for group practice built in.

So limiting the topic is very important. So is understanding who the audience will be, and whether what they need is education or skills.

If a group of support staff from different libraries have never gotten together before, nor had the chance to talk to each other about how tough life is on the front desk, a workshop structured to provide background information on the homeless problem in America—except in brief, clear, capsule form—is a waste of effort. What this group needs is a chance to share experiences, to talk about what works in certain situations and what doesn't, and the opportunity to acquire some specific new skills.

On the other hand, offering a workshop aimed at broadening the knowledge of youth services workers about the needs of immigrant children is a different kettle of fish entirely. Here a speaker providing overview information and analysis, coupled with presentations on different ideas for service, might be useful for everyone.

Hints for Organizing Better Workshops

First, make sure that everyone understands, up front, what the purpose of the workshop is, how it will be conducted, what will happen when, and where the restrooms are. Guarantee the time when breaks and lunch will occur, and stick to the announced schedule, even if this means interrupting a hot discussion (or if it's *really* hot, at least poll the participants before postponing a break). A third of the crowd will be grateful, I promise.

Plan the internal schedule of the workshop carefully, allowing plenty of flex time for discussions to run over without affecting breaks. Assume that it will not actually get started on time, but don't let the delay be more than ten minutes, or you risk annoying all the people who were prompt. Also assume that you will lose the audience, in spirit if not in fact, at 4 p.m., especially if the participants have come from someplace else, and are therefore worried about the evening commute home.

If the workshop is meant to teach skills, make sure the time allocations match the following general pattern: 15 percent for explaining the skill, 25 percent for demonstrating it, and 60 percent for engaging the trainees in guided practice.[4]

An "education" workshop, on the other hand, will spend far more time on lecturing, demonstration, discussion, and debate, with only perhaps 25 percent of the time allocated to small group work and consolidation of what has been learned.

If you are going to have a speaker, be careful whom you invite. Make sure someone whose judgment you trust has actually heard the speaker, and vouches for his or her effectiveness. Be sure that you and the speaker agree on both the methodology for teaching a skill, and how much time will be required. For example, I would look askance at anyone who offers to teach active listening skills in one hour, and proposes to do it via an overhead projector and handouts.

If the topic is broader, you will want to be sure that the speaker knows what is expected of her or him. Write it down in your confirmation letter, and be sure to include a description of who the participants are going to be. Nothing can ruin a workshop faster than a speaker who misjudges the audience, tells bad jokes about when-I-was-a-youngster-in-the-library, and rambles away from the point of the session.

Finally, move heaven and earth to find a workshop location that is big and comfortable enough — for both the whole group sessions and smaller groups. It is in accommodating the latter that so many workshop spaces are inadequate: four small groups meeting in the four corners of a room can be deafening for everyone. Look at how much time is going to be spent in small groups, and make acquiring space for that aspect a priority.

Introducing the New Manual

Closing down the library and holding an all day workshop for staff can be a lot of fun for everyone, and is the ideal way to introduce a new manual on handling problem situations. The staff committee which wrote the manual (see Chapter 9) can be assigned the task of organizing this event. Here's one scenario for just such a workshop.

Distribute the manual to every member of the staff two or three days, or even a week, before the workshop, with a request that they read it, and think about it. Many will not, of course, because they won't have time, but at least the document is in people's hands and has become somewhat familiar.

Open the workshop with a "nuts and bolts of the day" talk by the staff chair of the manual committee: the time of breaks, the arrangements for lunch, and so forth. Then introduce the director for a brief (ten minutes?) pep talk on the library's philosophy of service, what its behavior rules are, and the style the new manual uses in patron relations. It is very important that the imprimatur of official management support be given to the manual.

It is also important, and okay, to interrupt the director with the first of a series of demonstrations of difficult behavior, acted out by staff. For example, get a senior manager wearing a backwards baseball cap and a dirty tee shirt to skateboard down the center aisle of the meeting room, playing a boom box at top volume. How the director copes with the interruption (either badly or well) doesn't much matter, so long as everyone laughs, and listens to the explanation of how such an incident ought to be handled.

The rest of the day should be organized into the following pattern. Decide on the four or five most important sections of the manual, based on which problem situations are most difficult or frightening to staff. Then allocate a block of time for each of them. Introduce each difficult behavior with a role-played example, followed by a brief discussion with the audience of what was right or wrong about how the

incident was handled. Talk about the right way, and then break everyone into small groups (no more than six people) for fifteen minutes of
practice. Set the small groups up with three practice situations each
(they can be the same for all groups), ask people to act out the roles,
and discuss how each team handled the problem. If yours is a multibranch system, find a way to group people who work in branches of the
same size.

After the practice session, get everyone back together for questions, and for more explanation of the theory or background on the
problem. This is the moment, for example, for a member of the manual
committee to do five minutes on the problems caused by deinstitution-
alization of the mentally ill, and the local community's response.

Conclude the day with a final debriefing and question-and-answer
session. If serious problems about understanding a policy have emerged
during the day, try to deal with them here. It is best, of course, to end
on a high note — perhaps a final pep talk by the director. In Santa Cruz,
we traditionally end with wine and cheese. (But then, this is coastal
California.)

Role playing is a very important methodology for this kind of
workshop. As a training tool, it gives people experience and practice in
coping with problem situations, and in saying things which do not
necessarily come easily to them. Moreover, in small group practice
sessions, it is hard for even the shyest or most stubbornly silent person
to avoid participating.

As for the role playing which introduces each problem situation,
the more exalted the staff members acting out roles, the more fun all
the workshop participants will have. Few things in library life are more
enjoyable than watching the director of libraries make a fool of herself
pretending to be a street person who smells bad. And it can be a useful
experience for the head of youth services to act out the role of an
indignant parent who wants to know why on earth the library has a
copy of *Heather Has Two Mommies*.

Every library staff (indeed, every group of people) has its nay-say-
ers and negative talkers who do their best (or so the leader feels) to
sabotage the carefully constructed pattern of the meeting or training
session. They range from the ones who dominate the group by talking
too much to those who refuse to believe that a new procedure is going
to work, and stubbornly keep on saying so.

Cooper and Heenan, in *Preparing, Designing, and Leading Workshops*, offer smart advice for how to handle these kinds of problems,

which needn't be reiterated here. But this does bring up the continuing role of the manual committee. One thing the committee chair can say is, "You could be right. This may not work, although we think it will. But during the next year we are all going to be testing these procedures, and talking about how they work. What's the worst that can happen? If they don't work, we'll think up something better."

There are two points here. The first is that theoretically no procedures should be put into place without first testing them. And that is an easy rule to follow when the subject is a concrete one, such as how to register a borrower on the automation system. But people, and how they act, are not concrete. They are infinitely varied in their behavior, requiring flexibility of response by staff when the behavior causes a problem.

This means that while we can work out the best procedure we can think of, and run it by as many staff people as possible for comment before we "publish" it, we are never going to be certain that it is the best one until it has been used for a period of time. Therefore, we have to set up a mechanism for reporting on how the procedures in the new manual work, and evaluating those reports. And if procedures *don't* work, the committee has to be prepared to throw out even their very favorites, and start again.

The second point is the conclusion of this chapter and book. Problem situations in libraries seem to run a pattern. In fact, they are so usual they are boring. There will always be angry people, the occasional drunk, and kids who get too rambunctious. And there will be flashers, stalkers, molesters, babblers, stinkers, and people who want to challenge the contents of the collections. These we can anticipate, and train the staff to handle. It is the surprises which are the hard part, although they do keep library life interesting.

Fundamentally, these difficult times leave us with two options. We can allow ourselves to be frightened by a changing world, and reassure ourselves by setting up a barricade of rules and procedures. Or, we can accept the fact that problem situations — the aggravating but routine ones along with the unexpected — come with the territory, do our very best to prepare for both, and rely on our common sense, and that of our staffs, to handle whatever happens.

That's the course I urge. It's hard work. And the staff members and administrators who occupy the bedevilled territory of library work are in many ways the unsung heroines and heroes of the common culture. The territory in question is the people's place, even when they don't treat it right. It is the vital informational base for our evolving democracy. It is a territory which it is crucially necessary to hold open and free.

Perhaps the greatest irony in the situation is that as society's problems bear ever more strenuously on public libraries, the steps we take to make it possible for maximum use of the collections and resources by everybody will increasingly also bring complaints about our attempts to be even-handed.

Thus, the contradiction: Especially when we do the job well, there are fewer and fewer to thank us. We just have to remember that our work, in the aggregate, is of incalculable importance. Every day, libraries keep the nation's information in motion, keep the society literate and informed. Take libraries away from the people—all the people—and from the social process, and our nation would be in a very bad way indeed.

This book expresses my deep admiration and respect for library workers—sentiments that I know are shared throughout our profession. When times are tough, it's good to stop and remember that that comes with the territory too!

NOTES

1. Davies, Ivor K. *Instructional Technique*. New York: McGraw-Hill, 1981; p. 20.

2. Knowles, Malcolm. *The Adult Learner: A Neglected Species*, 3rd edition. Houston, Texas: Gulf Publishing, 1984; pp. 27–63.

3. Warncke, Ruth. *Planning Library Workshops and Institutes. The Public Library Reporter*, No. 17. Chicago: American Library Association, 1976.

Cooper, Susan, and Cathy Heenan. *Preparing, Designing, and Leading Workshops—A Humanistic Approach*. Boston: CBI Publishing, 1980.

4. Davies, p. 50.

Appendices

Appendices

Appendix A

THE LIBRARY BILL OF RIGHTS

The American Library Association affirms that all libraries are forums for information and ideas, and that the following basic policies should guide their services.

1. Books and other library resources should be provided for the interest, information, and enlightenment of all people of the community the library serves. Materials should not be excluded because of the origin, background, or views of those contributing to their creation.

2. Libraries should provide materials and information presenting all points of view on current and historical issues. Materials should not be proscribed or removed because of partisan or doctrinal disapproval.

3. Libraries should challenge censorship in the fulfillment of their responsibility to provide information and enlightenment.

4. Libraries should cooperate with all persons and groups concerned with resisting abridgement of free expression and free access to ideas.

5. A person's right to use a library should not be denied or abridged because of origin, age, background, or views.

6. Libraries which make exhibit spaces and meeting rooms available to the public they serve should make such facilities available on an equitable basis, regardless of the beliefs or affiliations of individuals or groups requesting their use.

Adopted June 18, 1948. Amended February 2, 1961, June 27, 1967, and January 23, 1980, by the ALA Council. Reprinted by permission of the American Library Association.

Appendix B

EXHIBIT SPACES AND BULLETIN BOARDS

An Interpretation of the *Library Bill of Rights*

Libraries often provide exhibit spaces and bulletin boards. The uses made of these spaces should conform to the *Library Bill of Rights*: Article I states, "Materials should not be excluded because of the origin, background, or views of those contributing to their creation." Article II states, "Materials should not be proscribed or removed because of partisan or doctrinal disapproval." Article VI maintains that exhibit space should be made available "on an equitable basis, regardless of the beliefs or affiliations of individuals or groups requesting their use."

In developing library exhibits, staff members should endeavor to present a broad spectrum of opinion and a variety of viewpoints. Libraries should not shrink from developing exhibits because of controversial content or because of the beliefs or affiliations of those whose work is represented. Just as librarians do not endorse the viewpoints of those whose works are represented in their collections, libraries also do not endorse the beliefs or viewpoints of topics which may be the subject of library exhibits.

Exhibit areas often are made available for use by community groups. Libraries should formulate a written policy for the use of these exhibit areas to ensure that space is provided on an equitable basis for all groups which request it.

Written policies for exhibit space use should be stated in inclusive rather than exclusive terms. For example, a policy that the library's exhibit space is open "to organizations engaged in educational, cultural, intellectual, or charitable activities" is an inclusive statement of the limited uses of the exhibit space. This defined limitation would permit religious groups to use the exhibit space because they engage in intellectual activities, but would exclude most commercial uses of the exhibit space.

A publicly supported library may limit use of its exhibit space to strictly "library-related" activities, provided that the limitation is clearly circumscribed and is viewpoint neutral.

Libraries may include in this policy rules regarding the time, place, and manner of use of the exhibit space, so long as the rules are content-neutral and are applied in the same manner to all groups wishing to use the space. A library may wish to limit access to exhibit space to groups within the community served by the library. This practice is acceptable provided that the same rules and regulations apply to everyone, and that exclusion is not made on the basis of the doctrinal, religious, or political beliefs of the potential users.

The library should not censor or remove an exhibit because some members of the community may disagree with its content. Those who object to the content of any exhibit held at the library should be able to submit their complaint and/or their own exhibit proposal to be judged according to the policies established by the library.

Libraries may wish to post a permanent notice near the exhibit area stating that the library does not advocate or endorse the viewpoints of exhibits or exhibitors.

Libraries which make bulletin boards available to public groups for posting notices of public interest should develop criteria for the use of these spaces based on the same considerations as those outlined above. Libraries may wish to develop criteria regarding the size of material to be displayed, the length of time materials may remain on the bulletin board, the frequency with which materials may be posted for the same group, and the geographic area from which notices will be accepted.

Adopted July 2, 1991, by the ALA Council. Reprinted by permission of the American Library Association.

Appendix C

MEETING ROOMS

An Interpretation of the *Library Bill of Rights*

Many libraries provide meeting rooms for individuals and groups as part of a program of service. Article VI of the *Library Bill of Rights* states that such facilities should be made available to the public served by the given library "on an equitable basis, regardless of the beliefs or affiliations of individuals or groups requesting their use."

Libraries maintaining meeting room facilities should develop and publish policy statements governing use. These statements can properly define time, place, or manner of use; such qualifications should not pertain to the content of a meeting or to the beliefs or affiliations of the sponsors. These statements should be available in any commonly used language within the community served.

If meeting rooms in libraries supported by public funds are made available to the general public for non-library sponsored events, the library may not exclude any group based on the subject matter to be discussed or based on the ideas that the group advocates. For example, if a library allows charities and sports clubs to discuss their activities in library meeting rooms, then the library should not exclude partisan political or religious groups from discussing their activities in the same facilities. If a library opens its meeting rooms to a wide variety of civic organizations, then the library may not deny access to a religious organization. Libraries may wish to post a permanent notice near the meeting room stating that the library does not advocate or endorse the viewpoints of meetings or meeting room users.

Written policies for meeting room use should be stated in inclusive rather than exclusive terms. For example, a policy that the library's facilities are open "to organizations engaged in educational, cultural, intellectual, or charitable activities" is an inclusive statement of the limited uses of the exhibit space. This defined limitation would permit religious groups to use the facilities because they engage in intellectual activities, but would exclude most commercial uses of the exhibit space.

A publicly supported library may limit use of its meeting rooms to strictly "library-related" activities, provided that the limitation is clearly circumscribed and is viewpoint neutral.

Written policies may include limitations on frequency of use, and whether or not meetings held in library meeting rooms must be open to the public. If state and local laws permit private as well as public sessions of meetings in libraries, the library may choose to offer both options. The same standard should be applicable to all.

If meetings are open to the public, libraries should include in their meeting room policy statement a section which addresses admission fees. If admission fees are permitted, libraries shall seek to make it possible that these fees do not limit access to individuals who may be unable to pay, but who wish to attend the meeting. Article V of the *Library Bill of Rights* states that "a person's right to use a library should not be denied or abridged because of origin, age, background, or views." It is inconsistent with Article V to restrict indirectly access to library meeting rooms based on an individual's or group's ability to pay for that access.

Adopted July 2, 1991, by the ALA Council. Reprinted by permission of the American Library Association.

Appendix D

GUIDELINES FOR THE DEVELOPMENT OF
POLICIES AND PROCEDURES REGARDING
USER BEHAVIOR AND LIBRARY USAGE

American Library Association Intellectual Freedom Committee

Introduction

Libraries are faced with problems of user behavior that must be addressed to insure the effective delivery of service and full access to facilities. Library governing bodies must approach the regulation of user behavior within the framework of the ALA Code of Professional Ethics, the *Library Bill of Rights* and the law, including local and state statutes, constitutional standards under the First and Fourteenth Amendments, due process and equal treatment under the law.

Publicly supported library service is based upon the First Amendment right of free expression. Publicly supported libraries are recognized as limited public forums for access to information. At least one federal court of appeals has recognized a First Amendment right to receive information in a public library. Library policies and procedures that could impinge upon such rights are subject to a higher standard of review than may be required in the policies of other public services and facilities.

There is a significant government interest in maintaining a library environment that is conducive to all users' exercise of their constitutionally protected right to receive information. This significant interest authorizes publicly supported libraries to maintain a safe and healthy environment in which library users and staff can be free from harassment, intimidation, and threats to their safety and well-being. Libraries should provide appropriate safeguards against such behavior and enforce policies and procedures addressing that behavior when it occurs.

In order to protect all library users' right of access to library facilities, to ensure the safety of users and staff, and to protect library resources and facilities from damage, the library's governing authority may impose reasonable restrictions on the time, place, or manner of library access.

Guidelines

The American Library Association's Intellectual Freedom Committee recommends that publicly supported libraries use the following guidelines, based upon constitutional principles, to develop policies and procedures governing the use of library facilities:

1. Libraries are advised to rely upon existing legislation and law enforcement mechanisms as the primary means of controlling behavior that involves public safety, criminal behavior, or other issues covered by existing local, state, or federal statutes. In many instances, this legal framework may be sufficient to provide the library with the necessary tools to maintain order.

2. If the library's governing body chooses to write its own policies and procedures regarding user behavior or access to library facilities, services, and resources, the policies should cite statutes or ordinances upon which the authority to make those policies is based.

3. Library policies and procedures governing the use of library facilities should be carefully examined to insure that they are not in violation of the *Library Bill of Rights*.

4. Reasonable and narrowly drawn policies and procedures designed to prohibit interference with use of the facilities and services by others, or to prohibit activities inconsistent with achievement of substantial library objectives, are acceptable.

5. Such policies and the attendant implementing procedures should be reviewed regularly by the library's legal counsel for compliance with federal and state constitutional requirements, federal and state civil rights legislation, all other applicable federal and state legislation, and applicable case law.

6. Every effort should be made to respond to potentially difficult circumstances of user behavior in a timely, direct, and open manner. Common sense, reason and sensitivity should be used to resolve issues in a constructive and positive manner without escalation.

7. Libraries should develop an ongoing staff training program based upon their user behavior policy. This program should include training to develop empathy and understanding of the social and economic problems of some library users.

8. Policies and regulations that impose restrictions on library access:
   a. should apply only to those activities that materially interfere with the public's right of access to library facilities, the safety of users and staff, and the protection of library resources and facilities;
   b. should narrowly tailor prohibitions or restrictions so that they are not more restrictive than needed to serve their objectives;
   c. should attempt to balance competing interests and avoid favoring the majority at the expense of individual rights, or allowing individual users' rights to supersede those of the majority of library users;
   d. should be based upon actual behavior and not upon arbitrary distinctions between individuals or classes of individuals. Policies should not target specific users or groups of users based

upon an assumption or expectation that such users might engage in behaviors that could disrupt library service;

e. should not restrict access to the library by persons who merely inspire the anger or annoyance of others. Policies based upon appearance or behavior that is merely annoying or which merely generates negative subjective reactions from others, do not meet the necessary standard unless the behavior would interfere with access by an objectively reasonable person to library facilities and services. Such policies should employ a reasonable, objective standard based on the behavior itself;

f. must provide a clear description of the behavior that is prohibited so that a reasonably intelligent person will have fair warning and must be continuously and clearly communicated in an effective manner to all library users;

g. to the extent possible, should not leave those affected without adequate alternative means of access to information in the library;

h. must be enforced evenhandedly, and not in a manner intended to benefit or disfavor any person or group in an arbitrary or capricious manner.

The user behaviors addressed in these guidelines are the result of a wide variety of individual and societal conditions. Libraries should take advantage of the expertise of local social service agencies, advocacy groups, mental health professionals, law enforcement officials, and other community resources to develop community strategies for addressing the needs of a diverse population.

Adopted January 24, 1993, by the American Library Association Intellectual Freedom Committee. Reprinted by permission of the American Library Association.

Appendix E

TWO SAMPLE EXHIBIT AND MEETING ROOM POLICIES

"Exhibit Policy," from Policy Manual,
Prince Georges County Memorial Library, Hyattsville, Maryland

A. The use of exhibit space in branch libraries is based on these criteria: visual arts, crafts, paintings, and collections for educational, cultural, informational, and artistic purposes. Exhibit space is available to community individuals and groups on an equitable basis, regardless of the beliefs or affiliations of those requesting space. Only exhibits which are attractive and neat will be accepted. The library reserves the right to reject an exhibit request based on the above criteria.

B. In order to make exhibit space available to as many community residents as possible, no individual or group should expect to provide an exhibit more than once a year within the library system.

C. The library does not provide insurance coverage for exhibit items. Exhibitors are responsible for providing coverage for items exhibited or exhibiting at their own risk.

D. For wall-mounted displays, the library will furnish wires, hooks, and a step ladder.

E. Sculptors must furnish their own pedestals.

F. Labels for exhibit items are to be furnished by the exhibitor. They must be neat and attractive; labels are to be attached to exhibit items. They are not to be taped on walls or exhibit cases. Prices may not be included on labels. No sales transactions may take place on library premises, but the exhibitor's telephone number and a short biographical sketch may be posted. If the telephone number is not posted, the library will not provide it to the public without express permission from the exhibitor.

G. The exhibitor is responsible for the installation and dismantling of display as scheduled.

H. If staff is forced to dismantle a display because the exhibitor has not removed it on time, the library system is not responsible for any damage.

I. Exhibits conform to the same regulations as outlined in . . . "Posting/ Distribution of Free Materials." Form of literature/displays determined to be unacceptable is: material of a commercial nature containing:

   a. Advertisements of products or services; prices of articles for sale
   b. Requests for contributions (including nonprofit or charitable institutions)
   c. Petitions or political literature supporting one cause or point of view
   d. Carelessly designed or untidy posters or brochures.

   J. Exhibits prepared by the *Library Staff* shall be prepared in a manner consistent with the *Library Bill of Rights,* especially Article II which states that "libraries should provide materials and information representing all points of view."

"Meeting Room Policy," from *Policy Handbook,* Santa Cruz (California) City County Library System

   The Santa Cruz City County Library System meeting rooms are available to nonprofit community groups and organizations in the areas served by the library branches. No group or organization will be permitted use of the room if it appears that the contemplated use would be a clear and present danger to the library, its occupants, or the community.

   1. The Library System and its affiliated organizations and programs have first priority for the use of meeting rooms. Government agencies have second priority and are charged no fees for use, but are expected to abide by other meeting room rules. Nonprofit community groups and organizations may reserve meeting room space on a first come, first served basis.

   2. Meeting rooms are reserved for the use of community and not-for-profit organizations only. No group whose purpose is commercial in nature may use library space, even if the planned event meets other use criteria.

   3. No group may reserve a room for more than twenty six (26) times in a single fiscal year or four days in a single month.

   4. No admission fee may be charged for any event; nor may collections be taken, funds solicited, or any direct sales made.

   5. All meetings held in library meeting rooms must be open to the public. A list of the scheduled meetings for a given week are posted by the Branch Manager.

   6. Attendance at a meeting may be no more than the maximum number of people certified by the Fire Department as the occupancy limit for each room. These are:

Aptos Branch:	69
Boulder Creek Branch:	34
Branciforte Branch:	35
Central Branch:	75
Scotts Valley Branch:	8

At the Aptos, Boulder Creek, and Central Branches, attendance must be at least ten (10). At the Branciforte and Scotts Valley Branches, where the meeting space is not designed for large groups, smaller meetings may be held.

7. Reservations must be made for specific hours, and groups must leave promptly at the conclusion of the specified time. Failure to cooperate with this rule will result in denial of future use privileges.

8. No bookings will be made for hours in which the branch is not open to the public, with exceptions at the following branches:

Aptos: Meetings may be booked until 10PM, provided the group's responsible person agrees to turn out all lights and ensure that the door is securely locked.

Central: No group may remain in the meeting room beyond the Branch's 9PM closing time. However, the Director of Libraries may waive this rule under special circumstances, upon request **in advance** by the group. An additional charge of $15.00 per hour for overtime security services by library staff will be made if permission is granted and volunteer staff are available.

9. None of the library branch meetings rooms are equipped for religious services, dances, or dramatic productions. Neither the Branciforte nor Scotts Valley Branches have suitable facilities for film showing. The Aptos, Boulder Creek, Branciforte, and Scotts Valley Branches have no public address systems, pianos, or other special equipment available for public use.

10. Loud talk or any use of the room which disturbs in any way the library or library users is prohibited.

11. Smoking is not permitted in any library facility. Alcoholic beverages may be served only with special permission, secured using procedures outlined in the Alcoholic Beverages Policy. Kitchenette facilities may be used only for light refreshments; no utensils are provided by the library.

12. No signs, posters, displays, or decorations may be put up without prior permission.

13. Groups are responsible for their own set-up of chairs, etc., and must clean up the room, returning it to the condition in which they found it, after completion of the meeting. Set up and clean up must occur **within the reserved time** for the meeting. Failure to cooperate with this rule will result in denial of future use privileges.

14. Groups will be held responsible for damages to any library facility, including furniture, carpeting, kitchenettes, or borrowed equipment.

15. Neither the name nor the address of the Santa Cruz City County Library System or any of its branches may be used as the address for groups or organizations using meeting rooms.

16. If a conflict arises over the interpretation of these regulations, the matter will be referred to the Library Oversight Committee.

17. Exceptions to this policy must be approved by the Library Oversight Committee. However, the Director of Libraries is granted power to waive rules if in her/his judgement emergency or other conditions warrant this action. The Director must report all such waivers to the Library Oversight Committee at its next regularly scheduled meeting.

Adopted: Santa Cruz Library Oversight Committee, November 3, 1988.

Appendix F

SAMPLE PROCEDURES AND POLICIES

The following pages contain the complete text of the Santa Cruz City County Library System's staff manual, *Handling Problem Situations in the Library — A Training and Reference Manual for Staff*.

Some policies and procedures from other libraries are also included. For convenience, they are interleaved in the Santa Cruz Manual, as noted in the Table of Contents, but in another typeface, for ease of differentiation.

AN IMPORTANT EMERGENCY PROCEDURE

If you cannot safely use the telephone to call 911, use the library automation system to request aid via E-Mail.

Log off using the LO command and hitting Return.

Press Return again.

At the Username prompt, enter EMERGENCY.
  You will not see a Password prompt or a $ prompt

At the MAIL prompt, type your message:

  CALL 911 FOR [BRANCH NAME]. SEND POLICE

ANY BRANCH READING AN EMERGENCY MESSAGE SHOULD IMMEDIATELY CALL 911 TO SEND LAW ENFORCEMENT ASSISTANCE TO THE BRANCH. ALSO, NOTIFY CENTRAL ADMINISTRATION OR THE PERSON IN CHARGE AT THE CENTRAL BRANCH

TABLE OF CONTENTS*

*The page numbers shown are of course adapted to reflect the pages that follow in the
present work.*

Problem Situations Defined

Problem situations, or **behavior** which **creates** a problem situation, are acts by library users which interfere with someone else's right to use the library.

> Problem behavior by library **users** is the specific subject of this manual, but it should be remembered that library staff and library equipment can also exhibit problem behavior. We do our best to ensure that staff do that as infrequently as possible. But occasional equipment glitches must be endured.

> This manual concerns problem situations created by people. Natural disasters, such as earthquake, flood, or fire, or physical injury are covered in the Emergency Plans for each Branch.

Library Policy

The cornerstone of the Santa Cruz City County Library System's user behavior policy is that no one has the right to interfere with anyone else's right to use the library. We try to make as few specific behavior rules as possible for two reasons:

- because the library is very serious about practicing tolerance for the differences among people — not just their race or ethnicity or age or sexual preference, but in their life styles and behaviors.

- because it is impossible to anticipate every behavior which might interfere with someone else's right to use the library.

It is also the Library's policy to enforce its standards of behavior as equitably as possible among people of all ages, all economic levels, and all appearances. We do not make judgements on the basis of how people look or dress, any more than we question their right to seek any information they wish.

Three Basic Rules

Respect, Courtesy, Calm, and Tact Are Our Watchwords

The Common Sense Rule Applies

Use Teamwork with Other Staff Whenever You Can

Staff should deal with the public with respect, courtesy, tact, and calm. It is important to understand that there is no simple "recipe" for solutions to all problems. Some people may cause problems by simply sitting and crying, while others are hostile, abusive, or even violent. The way in which the staff approaches the situation should depend to a large extent on the type of behavior the person is exhibiting. The next section of this manual contains specific coping techniques for **some**, but by no means all, of the situations which public library workers may experience.

Because of the uniqueness of each situation common sense should play a large part in any encounter. Common sense is defined by the dictionary as "sound and prudent (but often unsophisticated) judgment." Possessing common sense is a basic requirement for working in a public library. We may all be very sophisticated in our knowledge of computers or books, but it is our sound and prudent judgement which deals with a difficult drunk, or helps a child in distress. Read this manual and learn the procedures. But when in doubt, use your common sense.

Most workers' instincts will tell them when to be sympathetic or when to back off if a patron is potentially violent. But whatever the case, handling problems should involve teamwork: whenever you can, call on other staff to back you up.

Teamwork also means communicating with your colleagues. Often, staff can collectively develop effective responses to difficult situations or people if they share experiences, successes, and failures. Time and again it turns out that a person who has exhibited difficult behavior at one branch or one public desk, has done the same thing at another branch or desk. If the staff talks to one another, collective approaches can be devised.

MAKING THE BASIC RULES WORK

1. Don't ignore problems; they rarely go away.
2. Listen carefully and assess the situation.
3. Maintain a calm, nonjudgmental attitude.
4. Repeat the problem back to the person until you both agree on what the problem is.
5. When you understand what the problem is, take action, if you can, to resolve it.
6. Explain your position in firm, unambiguous language.
7. Avoid using a loud voice, or words which are moralizing or condescending.
8. State consequences.
9. Use teamwork.
10. Call outside help if necessary.
11. Communicate with your colleagues.

SPECIFIC COPING TECHNIQUES

1. The following pages describe specific coping techniques for handling various inappropriate behaviors.

2. The behaviors or problems are listed in alphabetical
   order.

3. Each subject starts with a box like this one, which gives
   a basic summary of what to do.

4. The summary is followed by more detailed explanation
   and discussion.

5. Three other Santa Cruz Library System Manuals are
   cited:

   The *Public Services Manual,* which contains all the
   Library System's policies, plus a lot of other information
   on how to do things.

   The *Branch Emergency Plan,* which has instructions for
   handling situations involving illness, injuries, and disasters of nature (fire, flood, earthquake).

   The *Blue Book* which describes all the procedures and
   policies associated with the automation system.

   Each of these manuals is available at your Branch.

Four Important Definitions

The Person in Charge is the senior person in the Branch at any given time,
unless (at Central) someone else is designated on the Schedule. In a smaller
Branch, the Person in Charge is usually the Branch Manager, but is whoever
the Branch Manager designates.

The Person in Charge has an absolute obligation to **stop** doing whatever she or
he is doing and cope with a problem situation if another staff person requests it.

> Be polite but firm: "I am sorry, but I must leave you to handle a
> problem which has just come up. So-and-so will help you in a minute
> [or] I will be back as soon as I can."

Law Enforcement is a single term for either the city police of Santa Cruz,
Capitola, or Scotts Valley, or the Sheriff's Department. All are reached from a

single Dispatcher at 911. However, in the City of Santa Cruz, the Santa Cruz Police can also be reached by dialing 3-911.

Community Backup is the person or persons (usually local merchants) with whom the Branch Manager of a facility in the unincorporated areas establishes a working security relationship. This is necessary because law enforcement response can be so slow when great distances must be travelled.

Incident Report Form: We use these forms to keep records of the problem situations which arise. They are good for collecting data on how often a difficult situation comes up, or the history of the Branch's encounters with a particularly troublesome problem. Do not fail to fill out an Incident Report. The City of Santa Cruz has special procedures for handling risk management issues. When an incident involves any one of the following things, **send the Incident Report to the Central Office within 24 hours, and do not keep a copy at the Branch:**

> Injury to a patron or staff member
>
> Damage to Library or patron property
>
> Need to call law enforcement

This applies to all Branches, no matter where they are located. The Central Office will file the City forms if required, or will return the Incident Report for the Branch's file.

ANGRY OR IRATE PEOPLE

1. Remain calm. Do not give the appearance of being combative, but do not appear fearful either.

2. Listen attentively and nod appropriately.

3. Speak slowly, clearly, and in a moderate tone of voice.

4. Take immediate action if you can.

5. If you can't achieve a resolution to the problem, pass the patron on to your supervisor.

Probably the problem situations library staff encounter most frequently are those involving people who are angry. Long experience among the staff has developed the following basic rules, and some special techniques.

1. Remain calm. Do not give the appearance of being combative but do not appear fearful either.

2. Listen attentively and elicit as much information as you can about the complaint. Nod appropriately. Not only does this communicate attentiveness to the patron, but it may help you relax.

3. Be aware of how you are speaking. Speak slowly and clearly and if you are using a loud tone, lower your voice.

4. Be aware, also, that other library patrons are listening. What you say to the angry patron will be judged by people who are not involved. A demeanor of calm and reason keeps other listeners on the library's side, and conveys information about library policies.

5. When you understand what the problem is, take some immediate action. If the patron's complaint is legitimate, do something immediately to remedy the situation. For example, if a patron is complaining about a long wait for a Request, check to see where the patron stands on the list, give her/him this information, and say how many copies of the item we have purchased.

6. If you can't achieve a satisfactory resolution to the problem, pass the patron on to your supervisor or to System Administration.

The Paraphrasing Technique

In many arguments, but especially those involving emotional issues, one of the problems is that the combatants don't listen to each other. One side is busy preparing her/his rebuttal while the other side is still speaking.

The paraphrasing technique is useful because it ensures that both sides really listen. They have to in order to restate the other person's position.

1. As the angry patron states her/his problem, feed back the patron's own words by repeating what has been said (paraphrase).

2. Once you have paraphrased the patron's previous statement, secure confirmation from the patron that your paraphrase is an accurate restatement of what was said.

3. If the patron says your paraphrase was not accurate, try again until you get agreement. Or, ask the patron to restate the point. Paraphrase again until you have done so to the patron's satisfaction.

4. State the library's position only when your paraphrasing has been accepted by the patron.

5. When the patron wants to speak again, she/he must accurately paraphrase you and receive **your** agreement before speaking.

Here's an example of what a staff person might say when dealing with a user who is angry about an overdue video fine.

Patron: I think it is outrageous that you charge $3.00 per day for an overdue video. I thought the overdue fine was 25 cents like everything else.

Staff:	You don't like the $3.00 per day overdue fine for videos, and you didn't know about it, is that what you're saying?
Patron:	Yes, that's right. I didn't know.
Staff:	Well, the daily overdue fine charge is printed on the video box, and there is a date due slip too. We charge $3.00 per day to get people to bring the videos back when they are due. We don't have very many videos, and a lot of people want to use them.
Patron:	I don't care. I think $3.00 is way too much to charge.
Staff:	You don't think our $3.00 charge is fair, is that right? Well, do you understand **why** we make the charge?
Patron:	Yes, I guess so. But I think it is way too much.
NOTE:	Often, you are not going to be able to get a user to actually repeat back what you have said. The most important point is to get the user to agree that she/he understands that there are two points of view, one of which is yours. So you should **ask** the user if she/he understands, and if she/he doesn't, start again.

The Stand and Deliver Technique

Sometimes a patron is too angry for paraphrasing to work. The patron is furious, and wants a chance to express her/his rage to someone from the library. No staff person needs to listen to abusive or obscene language from a library user (see VERBAL ABUSE OF STAFF), but there is a technique for handling other people who are angry. We call this the "Stand and Deliver Technique" because the staff person stands there and the patron delivers his/her anger.

1. Remain calm. Do not give the appearance of being combative but do not appear fearful either.

2. Listen attentively and nod appropriately.

3. Don't attempt to respond to the patron. If you do, the patron will simply interrupt you. For the moment, just stand there nodding and murmuring affirmative sounds appropriately.

4. Eventually, the patron will talk herself out. When she does, state the library's position on the patron's problem.

5. Work hard to keep yourself from arguing with the patron; simply restate the library's policy over and over.

6. While remaining firm, try to find alternatives that will mitigate the situation without violating policy. Perhaps you can even ask the patron to help you think of acceptable alternatives.

7. If, after following these guidelines, the angry patron still will not let go, call the Person in Charge. If you are the Person in Charge, refer the patron to

the Director of Libraries. Often angry people will respond more positively to "the boss."

Requests for Special Treatment

If the patron's complaint is **not** legitimate and she/he wants you to make a special exception for her/him, or alter established policy, you need to be firm. Explain the library's policy and show the patron a written copy of it if necessary.

A typical example of this kind of behavior is a patron who wants you to lend him/her a reference book to take out of the branch to copy at a cheaper copy shop, or to use at home overnight.

User: Come on! You **know** me. I've been using this Branch for five years. I'm not going to **steal** it. Let me have it to take to Kinko's, and I promise I'll have it back by 5PM.

Staff: I'm sorry, but I am really not able to do that. I know **you** wouldn't steal it, but if I let you take it, I have to let everyone take it, and not everyone is as honest as you are.

User: But you know the kind of people who are going to steal something.

Staff: That's the point. Then I would be in the position of making **judgments** about people, and I am not able to do that.

COLLECTION DEVELOPMENT AND SELECTION POLICY
Monroe County Public Library, Bloomington, Indiana

Materials Evaluation Policy. In order to insure effective communication between the library and the community concerning the range of ideas and information and inclusive portrayals of human experience in the library collection, the library maintains a materials evaluation procedure.

This procedure is as follows:

1. When a member of the community has a question or an objection concerning the presence of a book or other item in the collection, library staff will listen to the question or objection and inform the person of the library's policy on collection development, especially the following paragraph:

"Materials included in the collection present all points of view on current and historical issues and inclusive portrayals of human experience in a wide variety of media and styles. The origin, background, or viewpoint of an author does not exclude the author's work from the collection. Partisan or doctrinal disapproval does not result in exclusion or removal of a work from the collection. The origin, age, background, or viewpoint of a library user does not deny or abridge that person's right to full use of the library."

2. If this discussion does not satisfy the patron, the staff member will offer the patron a Materials Evaluation Form and encourage the patron to fill out the form. This form should be completed as fully as possible and returned to the Department Head where the initial contact was made for forwarding directly to the Director's office.

3. Upon receipt of the Materials Evaluation Form, the Director will convene a Materials Evaluation Committee consisting of the Department Head where the concern originated, the staff person who made the original selection decision, a member of the staff that would add expertise to the committee, and the Director as Chairperson of the Committee.

4. All members of the Committee will read, view, or listen and evaluate the material in question.

5. The Committee will then meet to discuss and evaluate the material and the Materials Evaluation Form. The Director will prepare a report summarizing the Committee's evaluation and a copy will be sent to the person who submitted the Materials Evaluation Form.

6. If the concerned patron is not satisfied with the Materials Evaluation Committee's report, he/she can request a hearing with the library's Board of Trustees. At this point the Board members will be sent a copy of the Committee's report and a copy of the Materials Evaluation Form.

BOOK COMPLAINTS AND
QUESTIONS ABOUT LIBRARY MATERIALS

1. Use friendly questioning to establish the nature of the patron's concern.
2. If you do not feel you can handle a library materials question well, pass the patron on to your supervisor right away.
3. Make sure the patron knows the library has other materials in the subject area.
4. Explain that the professional staff selects materials on the basis of the Collection Development Plan and the Library Bill of Rights.
5. Ask the patron to fill out a Comment Form so that a senior librarian can respond.

Library staff are very sensitive about issues concerning what we call "intellectual freedom": attempts by members of the public, elected officials, or anyone else to censor the materials in the library. So we can respond defensively when anyone challenges a particular book or other item.

On the other hand, most people who raise questions about a book or other item don't think of themselves as censors and they don't believe in censorship. They simply don't like specific materials, and want to be able to tell somebody (i.e. a library staff person) about it.

Thus the staff's object in handling a question or complaint about library materials is to ensure that the individual has the opportunity to talk out what she/he thinks, that she/he knows the full range of materials the library offers in the subject area, and that she/he understands the library's procedures for selecting materials.

The outcome of a patron complaint may in the end be the person filling out a Library Materials Comment Form, but this should happen only after the staff person has worked to achieve the objectives above.

1. If an individual questions the selection of library materials (either a specific book or other item, or the policy in general), question her/him in a friendly and neutral way to establish the exact nature of the objection. Stay calm and remember that everyone has a right to an opinion.

    If you do not feel that you can handle this kind of situation effectively, pass the person on to your Branch Manager or the Person in Charge.

2. Make sure the individual knows that the library has other material in the subject area.

3. Explain that the professional library staff is responsible for selecting library materials, and that it uses a Collection Development Plan for this.

4. Explain that the basis of our policy is the Library Bill of Rights and the Freedom to View Statement of the American Library Association. The library's job is to provide materials and information presenting all points of view on current and historical issues. This applies to both written documents and audiovisual materials.

    Copies of the Library Bill of Rights and the Freedom to View Statement are in the Public Services Manual. Each Branch Manager has a copy of the Collection Development Plan.

5. If the person persists in complaining about a specific item, ask her/him to fill out a Library Materials Comment Form. This is available in this manual, in the Public Services Manual or get one from your Supervisor/Branch Manager. Be sure that the form is filled out completely. If necessary, explain to the complaining patron that the staff does not respond to complaints about library materials without a written Comment Form.

6. Give the completed Library Materials Comment Form to your Branch

Manager who will pass it on to the Assistant Director. One of the System Coordinators or the Assistant Director will telephone or write to the complainant.

HERE'S AN EXAMPLE OF ONE KIND OF COMPLAINT, WITH ADDED INFORMATION ON HOW THE STAFF HANDLED IT. IT IS A TRUE STORY.

Man arrives at Central Branch Children's Room Desk and slaps down three books.

Patron: I can't believe you have these kinds of books in your children's collections. Look at this [he picks one up]: *What Happens to a Hamburger.* And this: *About the Foods You Eat.* I have never seen anything more biased. These are encouraging children to kill animals. I don't think the library should have books like this!

Staff: You object to these books being in the library collection, is that it?

User: I certainly do. And what is **this**, *The Natural Cook's First Book*? We ought to be training our children to eat vegetables instead of chicken and eggs and milk. I'm serious. I think the library is criminal to promote viewpoints which endanger health and the whole planet.

Staff: Actually, having a book on the shelves isn't promoting it. Our job is to provide information on all things, including different sets of beliefs. And I know we have some books on vegetarianism. Let's look in the catalog for them, shall we?

User: But it is wrong to teach children to disregard their own health.

Staff: The library has a policy for selecting books and all our materials. It is called the Library Bill of Rights, and it says that the library's job is to provide materials and information presenting all points of view on issues. I can give you a copy if you'd like to read it.

User: Well, that may be, but what I want to know is who bought **these** books. Did the person know any better?

Staff: The professional library staff selects all our materials, based on our Collection Development Plan, and on the Library Bill of Rights. If you want to know why the staff picked these particular books, you need to fill out this form. Here's a copy of the form and also a copy of the Library Bill of Rights.

User: No, I don't **want** to do one of your forms. I just want you to know I think it is outrageous to have books like these on the shelves for children. We should be teaching them what is healthy, not how to poison their bodies. Here: I have a list of four books which would be much better for you to own.

Staff: The staff will be interested to hear your comments on the books, and whoever is responsible for that part of the collection will send you a written response. But you do have to fill out the form if you

LIBRARY MATERIALS COMMENT FORM

LIBRARY BRANCH: _____ DATE: _____

AUTHOR: _____

TITLE: _____

PUBLISHER: _____

DATE OF PUBLICATION: _____ CALL NUMBER: _____

WHAT BROUGHT THIS ITEM TO YOUR ATTENTION? (reviews, word-of-mouth, etc.)

_____

IF REVIEWS, PLEASE GIVE THE NAME AND DATE OF PUBLICATIONS, IF POSSIBLE:

_____

HAVE YOU READ/REVIEWED THE ENTIRE ITEM? _____ TO WHAT DO YOU
OBJECT? (Please be specific, citing pages if possible.)

_____

_____

continue on reverse if more space is needed

YOUR NAME: _____ PHONE: _____

COMPLETE ADDRESS: _____

_____

REPRESENTING SELF? _____

REPRESENTING ORGANIZATION? NAME: _____

_____

SIGNATURE

Appropriate Library staff will give careful consideration to the points you raise, and will respond in writing as soon as possible.

FOR STAFF USE ONLY

Date Received:	Assigned to:
Date Completed:	
Copies to:	Branch Manager, Coord or AD, Director

5/15/92 OFFICE\MATCOMM.FRM

want them to consider your opinion. You do that, and I'll clip your suggestion list to it.

OUTCOME: The Youth Services Coordinator wrote the patron a letter explaining that the library endeavors to present all sides on issues. She said that she had reviewed the books he complained about, and that she was satisfied that they fairly represented the view that chicken, eggs, milk, and meats are part of a balanced diet.

         She went on to point out two books in the Live Oak Children's Branch describing a vegetarian lifestyle. And she invited him to suggest other titles for purchase, commenting that all four of the titles he had listed were written for adults, rather than children.

The Library Materials Reconsideration Process

The Branch Manager sends the Library Materials Comment Form [see pages 156–157] on to the Assistant Director. She copies it for the Director, and sends it to the Youth Services Coordinator, the Reference Coordinator, or to a selection librarian. Who handles responding to the Comment depends on the subject of the material. The staff person assigned tries to reach the patron by telephone to clarify the exact nature of the complaint. A written response or a follow up to the phone call is mailed within two weeks.

A patron who wishes to complain or comment further about a specific item:

1. Must write a letter to the Director of Libraries, who will review the documentation, and respond within two weeks.

2. May write an appeal of the Director of Libraries decision to the Chair of the Library Oversight Committee, who will schedule the matter on the agenda of the next regular meeting of the Library Oversight Committee. Part of the Agenda consideration will be a report from the staff.

CHATTY PEOPLE WHO DISTRACT STAFF

1. Be polite, but discourage long conversations.

2. Be direct in stating that you must do other work.

3. Help other staff members trapped in this situation by intervening if you can.

---

1. Chatty people are sometimes lonely people, and the staff should be tolerant of their behavior and needs.

2. Be polite, but discourage long irrelevant conversations with people.

3. If a person continues a lengthy conversation, politely explain that it is necessary to return to work or to help another patron.

EXAMPLE:

Staff: Look, it's been fun talking with you, but I do have work to do for other people. Thanks for coming in.

4. Other staff members should be aware of situations like this, and intervene to help their colleague break up the conversation.

    If there are two phone lines, try calling your trapped colleague.

CHILD ABUSE BY PARENTS OR CAREGIVERS

1. Intervene if you can to protect the child, but do not endanger yourself.

2. Try to distract the angry adult.

3. Try to get the name of the adult.

Incidents of adults (parents or other caregivers) physically abusing children in the library are surprisingly frequent. "Abuse" is defined as a physical act designed to hurt the child, including repetitive slapping, excessive spanking, and arm twisting.

Adults who abuse children are very angry. They could easily turn on a staff member who intervenes, and physically attack. Or, they could increase their attack on the child, or later blame the child for staff intervention.

Therefore, the objective in a library staff intervention has to be distracting the adult to bring the immediate abuse to a stop.

It is unclear under California law whether library workers are under the same obligation as teachers and childcare workers to report cases of suspected (or observed) child abuse. Therefore, our Library System's policy is to document each observed case, to try to determine the name and address of the adult and the child, and to consult with caseworkers at the Office of Child Protective Services.

1. If you observe an incident of child abuse, or suspect that one is occurring in the children's restroom, intervene to try to distract the adult, if you can do so safely.

2. Do not physically get between the adult and the child.

3. Use language which objectifies the situation, such as
   "We don't allow hitting in the library."

4. **Do not** use language which accuses the adult, such as
   "We don't allow child abuse in the library," or
   "You stop hitting that child."

5. If the parent says something like,
   "Don't you interfere with me. This is my child. I can treat it any way I want . . ."

   respond (keeping your voice very calm) by saying,
   "I'm trying to make sure other library users aren't disturbed. Can I help you in any way?"

6. Try to obtain the name and address of the adult.

7. Write up a description on an Incident Form as soon as possible.

8. Discuss the incident with your Branch Manager before proceeding. If you are the Branch Manager, consult with the Youth Services Coordinator about what to do.

DULUTH PUBLIC LIBRARY, LIBRARY POLICY ON UNATTENDED, LOST, OR MISSING CHILDREN

Statement of Purpose

It is the intention of this policy to enlist the cooperation of parents and other adults responsible for children to ensure that the Duluth Public Library provides a safe and pleasant experience for all who use it.

Policy Statement

Parents/guardians may not leave children age seven and under unattended in the library. Parents/guardians are responsible for their children's behavior while in the library.

Child Left Unattended

1. Children left unattended are often frightened and crying and should be comforted by staff.

2. If it is determined that a child is lost or left unattended, a staff member

should try to identify and locate the parent/guardian or responsible adult, according to the following procedure:

A. Walk around the children's area with the child, looking for the parent/ guardian.

B. Page the child's parent/guardian using the name if known, or the child's name, if known. If no name is available, describe the child's physical appearance.

C. When an adult is located, explain the library policy on unattended children.

D. If the parent/guardian is not found in the building, a staff member should stay with the child until someone can be located, through searching the database, phone book, city directory, etc.

E. If the parent/guardian has not been located within an hour, or if the Library is closing, the staff member will call the police.

F. Under no circumstances will a staff member take the child out of the building.

Child Reported Missing or Lost

If a parent/guardian reports a child age seven or under missing, staff will follow this procedure:

A. Obtain name, age, and description of child. Ask parent/guardian how extensively they have searched. Check children's area thoroughly, including bathrooms and offices.

B. Request assistance from Circulation and Popular Library staff to search their areas.

C. If unable to locate child on Superior Street floor, page staff on other floors to request their assistance. Provide a description of the child. Check elevator.

D. Check outside the library.

E. Call police if unable to locate the child.

CHILDREN LEFT UNATTENDED

1. Comfort a frightened child.

2. Attempt to locate the parent or caregiver.

3. If found, firmly explain the Library's "no-unattended" policy.

4. If the Library is closing, follow procedures in your Branch's Emergency Plan. Write these in here:

---

1. Children separated from or left unattended by their parents are often frightened and may be crying. They should be comforted by staff.

2. If it is determined that a child is lost or has been left unattended, take the child to the Young People's room staff at Central or to the Branch Manager at other Branches. Notify the Person in Charge.

3. The Young People's room staff or Branch Manager should try to identify or locate the parents or responsible person, and when located, firmly explain the library's policy on unattended children.

    CHILDREN UNDER 9 MUST BE SUPERVISED BY A PERSON
    14 YEARS OF AGE OR OLDER

4. If the library is closing and the parents or responsible adults have not returned for their child, or cannot be contacted, the Person in Charge should follow the procedure outlined in the Branch's Emergency Manual.

5. Staff should remain with the child until appropriate arrangements have been made.

6. Under no circumstances should a staff member drive the child home.

7. If the child is taken to another place (the Fire Station, the Police Station, etc.), leave a note on the door stating where and at what time the child was taken.

8. If the child is taken to another place, fill out an Incident Report, and send it to the Central Office within 24 hours.

COMPLAINTS OR QUESTIONS ABOUT LIBRARY POLICIES

1. Remember that everyone has a right to question or complain.

2. Remain calm and nonjudgmental.

3. Use paraphrasing to find out what the question or complaint is really about.

4. Take action if you can.

5. Refer the person to your Branch Manager or someone higher up if you can't satisfy them.

All library users have a right to question general library procedures and policies. When such situations arise, staff members should:

1. Remain calm and be receptive and nonjudgmental.

2. Listen carefully to the patron's question or complaint.

3. Use paraphrasing to establish the exact nature of the complaint, and pause and think before responding.

4. Clearly explain the library's policy and show a written copy of it to the patron if necessary. Remember to explain *why* we have a particular policy.

5. If you don't know the answer, say so, and refer the patron to someone who does. Being frank about your ignorance is always better than trying to fake it.

   "I'm sorry, Mrs. Jones. I've never worked in the cataloging department, so I don't know all the different things which go into setting the processing cost for a lost book. But I know our Branch Manager, Susie Smith, does. She comes in at noon today and is working tonight. Can I ask her to call you?"

6. In explaining policy, it is nice if all staff take grammatical responsibility for the library's policies. That is, try to refer to "we" rather than "they."

7. Follow through with action, trying to find alternatives if possible.

8. If necessary, refer the patron to another worker or to the Person in Charge.

9. If the person is still not satisfied, refer her/him to the Branch Manager, the appropriate Coordinator, the Assistant Director, or the Director.

Here's an example of what a staff person might say when dealing with a new user who is angry about the driver's license requirement:

Staff: What I hear you saying is: "I don't see why I need a driver's license just to get a library card." Is that what you're saying?

User: Yes. Why should I have a driver's license to use the library? I'm a
           taxpayer. I should be able to check out anything I want.

Staff: You're saying, "I don't see why I need a driver's license to get a
           library card, because you are a taxpayer, and you should be able to
           check out anything." Is that right?

User: YES, that's just what I said!

Staff: Okay, here's the reason. We require a driver's license because the
           DMV is the only way we have to find people who move and take
           the library's books with them. It is just like how you have to show
           your driver's license to write a check, but with the library, you only
           have to do it once.

User: Huh!

Staff: So do you understand why we are requiring DMV identification?

User: I guess so.

For additional guidelines, see ANGRY OR IRATE PATRON

MONROE COUNTY PUBLIC LIBRARY
303 East Kirkwood Avenue
Bloomington, IN 47408-3592
339-2271
PATRON COMMENT

Patron Name (Please print) _____

Address   _____   Phone # _____

_____   Zip _____

Patron represents (check one):
_____   himself/herself
_____   name of group or organization   _____

1. State Problem (Be specific; cite relevant department, service, or policy.)
   _____

2. Are you familiar with the official library policy/procedures covering
   this situation?
   _____

3. Is this your first encounter with this problem?

4. State suggestions for improvement: _____
   _____

_____   Signature: _____

_____   Date: _____

Taken by: _____
                     (staff member)
                  MAIN _____ ELL _____ BKM _____

Response   Date

DISRUPTIVE BEHAVIOR

1. Approach the person(s) (adult, young adult, or child) and tell him/her that his/her behavior is inappropriate.

2. Be polite, be specific, and state consequences.
   "When you talk loudly, it disturbs other people. Please lower your voice or you will have to leave the library."

3. Get backup from other staff if you have trouble.

4. If a second warning doesn't work, ask the patron(s) to leave.

5. If they won't leave, call law enforcement.

"Disruptive behavior" is usually not physically threatening, but is nonetheless disturbing to other library users. It can occur either inside or outside the library. Examples include a person audibly cursing, two people having a loud argument, a group of teenagers engaging in horse play, or children pounding on the windows from outside the building.

Other users are not always quick to report disruptive people, so be alert to signs that a patron behaving inappropriately is disturbing other people. The signs include:

- Patrons moving away from another patron.
- Patrons staring at another patron.
- Patrons looking at staff members.

1. If a patron disrupts library users or staff (whether intentionally or not), approach the person, explain that the behavior is inappropriate in the library and ask the patron(s) to stop at once. Explain what the patron is doing which is disruptive, and say what the consequences will be if she/he does not stop.

   "When you curse out loud like that, it really bothers other people. Is there something I can help you with? Please do stop swearing, or you will have to leave the library."

2. Groups of children who become noisy should be told in a firm, but nice, way that their behavior is inappropriate in a library and is disturbing to others.

   "Kids, when you run up and down the stack aisles like that, it frightens older people, and is dangerous. Please stop it right now. If you don't, I'll have to ask you to leave."

3. Groups of teenagers who are acting out need to be handled calmly but firmly. Be direct and concrete about what they are doing which disturbs other people. Do not show fear or allow yourself to be side tracked or intimidated. Never physically touch a young person. Resist the temptation to isolate the group's leader and embarrass him or her.

4. If the group or person continues to be disruptive, give a second warning, restating the consequences. Get backup from a co-worker.

5. If you are not the Person in Charge, tell that person what is going on.

6. If the second warning is not effective, ask the person or group to leave the library. If they refuse, explain that you will call law enforcement. Then do it if necessary.

7. Write an Incident Report for your Branch's file. If a person is injured, property is damaged, or law enforcement is called, send the Incident Report to the Central Office within 24 hours.

Added Instructions for Handling Disruptive Children

1. When a parent or other caregiver is present, but fails to correct disruptive behavior by their child, don't hesitate to speak directly to the child yourself. Try to avoid physically touching a child, except of course to protect the child's safety.

2. If the behavior continues, tell the parent that his/her child is disturbing others, and that the library holds parents responsible for the behavior of their children.

   Do not let yourself be intimidated by a parent who believes you have misjudged or unfairly "disciplined" his/her child. If the parent complains about your treatment, refer her/him to your supervisor, or ask them to write out their complaint. Tell the parent that your supervisor will respond by telephone or in writing.

3. Parent use of the library as a temporary baby-sitting service should be dealt with firmly. Tell parents that the library does not provide such a service and cannot be responsible for their children. Point out the library's posted rule that children under 9 must be supervised by a person 14 years of age or older.

4. Programs for children (story hours and the like) inevitably draw lots of kids who are excited and thus noisy. Should an adult patron complain, respond sympathetically, explain the circumstances, and try to be specific about when things might calm down.

   "Yes, I know it is noisy right now. They are having a special mask-making program in the Children's Room, and everyone is very excited. It should be over in another half hour. We are trying to keep a lid on, but you know how kids are."

Added Instructions for Handling Groups of Young Adults

1. We encourage pre-teens and teenagers to use the library and its resources for working on school and other projects. And we understand that young people are often most comfortable working in groups. This does not mean, however, that young adults can interfere with other people's ability to use the library.

2. When we have a group of "regulars" who are causing continuing problems, the Branch Manager or the Branch's Youth Services Librarian should try contacting the appropriate school for help in talking to the youngsters or reaching parents.

3. Taking Polaroid pictures of rowdy kids is a useful means for identifying them to school officials.

See also CHILDREN LEFT UNATTENDED
              DRUNKENNESS
              EMOTIONALLY/MENTALLY DISTURBED PATRON

PROCEDURE FOR HANDLING PERSONS SUSPECTED OF BEING UNDER THE INFLUENCE OF ALCOHOL OR DRUGS
from *Customer Relations Manual*, Ontario (California) City Library

Persons under the influence of alcohol can generally be detected by their alcoholic breath, but it is often difficult to determine the presence of drugs when a person is behaving in an aberrant manner. Such behavior may also be caused by physiological disorders. In either case, exercise caution in approaching such persons, since the person may exhibit sudden and extreme mood changes. (California Penal Code Sec. 647f.)

Staff Procedure

1) Get another staff member to serve as back-up support. Have a pre-arranged signal for calling the Police.

2) Remember to look for a medical alert tag.

3) Do not make the person feel watched or cornered. Stay at a safe distance. *Do not* touch the person.

4) If you need to assist the person with locating library materials, do not go alone with him/her to remote areas of the library.

5) If the person cannot function normally, ask the person calmly, "Are you ill? Do you need medical assistance?" Call the Paramedics at 9-911 if needed.

6) At the first sign of dangerous behavior, call or have a colleague call 9-911.

7) If the customer is disruptive, ask him/her to stop. Give warning that if the behavior continues she/he will be asked to leave the library.

8) If the customer persists, obtain the support of other staff and ask the customer to leave the library.

9) If the customer refuses to leave, call Police at 9-911.

10) If the situation warrants, fill out a Customer Incident form.

DRUG AND CHEMICAL DEPENDENCY PROBLEMS

1. Get backup from another staff person if you can.

2. Ask disruptive people to leave the Library.

4. Do not make the person feel threatened by standing close to them, and do not touch the person.

5. Call law enforcement for assistance.

STAFF WITNESSING THE SALE OR USE OF ILLEGAL DRUGS ARE REQUIRED TO NOTIFY LAW ENFORCEMENT AT ONCE.

It is not always obvious whether a person who is acting strangely is under the influence of drugs or suffering from a more permanent psychological problem. Whatever the case, if the person is interfering with other people's right to use the library by being disruptive, he/she must be asked to leave.

1. If you need help in dealing with an individual, get backup from a co-worker. At a larger Branch, consult with the Person in Charge. If you are on your own at a smaller Branch, be cautious in your approach; solicit help from other patrons if this seems appropriate.

2. Be careful not to make the patron feel threatened, as this will only make the situation worse. Do not touch him or her.

3. If the patron refuses to leave, or is incapable of leaving, call for law enforcement help.

4. A staff member or patron who witnesses the use or sale of illegal drugs should notify law enforcement at once.

5. Write an Incident Report for your Branch's file. If a person is injured, property is damaged, or law enforcement is called, send the Incident Report to the Central Office within 24 hours.

DRUNKEN BEHAVIOR

1. Drunks can be dangerous and should be approached carefully.

2. Get backup help from a co-worker, and tell a disruptive drunk to leave the library.

3. If the person seems dangerous, call law enforcement immediately.

When people smell of alcohol, staff need to exercise judgment in deciding how to handle the situation. If the patron's behavior is not otherwise offensive, then there is no problem. If, on the other hand, the patron is noticeably intoxicated, loud, obnoxious, or if other patrons are complaining, action needs to be taken.

1. If you get into an argument (about an overdue book, or the length of wait on the Reserve List, etc.) with a patron who smells of alcohol, be extra careful in your ANGRY OR IRATE PATRON handling technique. Probably the best approach is "Stand and Deliver"—don't argue, just listen. State the Library's point, and remember that the patron won't be so angry when she/he is sober.

2. People who are obviously drunk can be dangerous and should be approached carefully.

3. If the person seems dangerous, call law enforcement immediately. Don't worry about providing warning.

4. Get back-up help from co-workers and ask the individual to leave the building, because "Your behavior is inappropriate in the library."

5. If the individual refuses to leave warn the individual that the police will be called.

6. If the problem persists and the individual will not leave, or is unable to leave, call law enforcement.

7. In the City of Santa Cruz, it is illegal to carry open bottles of alcohol.

8. Write an Incident Report for your Branch's file. If a person is injured, property is damaged, or law enforcement is called, send the Incident Report to the Central Office within 24 hours.

EATING OR DRINKING IN THE LIBRARY

1. Explain the rule against eating or drinking inside the Library.

2. Tell the person where they can eat or drink.

If a person is consuming food or beverages in the Library, or has an open container, approach the individual and explain the Library's policy. Suggest that the person finish the food or drink outside or in the lobby. If the person doesn't stop, ask him or her to leave the Library.

> "Excuse me, Sir. The Library has an absolute rule against eating or drinking inside the building. You will need to take that to the lobby or outside right now to finish it. Thanks."

This is the kind of situation which on a bad day can escalate into a difficult encounter. Be polite, stay calm, and be flexible. Coffee, soft drinks, and alcohol get spilled and mess up the rugs, tables, and library materials. Donuts and other messy food can do the same thing, and also attract bugs, which you might want to point out to the patron. The rule was written to prevent accidents with these kinds of food and drink. But a candy bar is not worth fussing about. The Common Sense Rule applies.

PROCEDURE FOR HANDLING ABERRANT BEHAVIOR AND EMOTIONALLY DISTURBED PERSONS
from *Customer Relations Manual,* Ontario (California) City Library

Aberrant Behavior: General

Behavior defined as aberrant in this section is usually caused by psychological problems or substance abuse. Examples are talking to oneself, pacing the aisles, staring, unsteady walking and overly loud talking.

Please be aware that some medical conditions, e.g., diabetes, may cause symptoms similar to those normally associated with intoxication.

Staff Procedure

1) If the aberrant behavior is not disturbing other customers or staff, it should be tolerated.

2) Do not touch the customer, but visually check for a medical alert

tag around wrist or neck. If the customer is able to function and does not need assistance, treat him/her as you would any other customer.

3) If the customer appears to be ill or to need personal assistance, ask if you can be of help. Offer to call either the Paramedics at 9-911 or a family member if it is not an emergency.

4) If the person becomes disruptive, follow the procedures outlined in the section on "Disruptive Behavior," incorporating the special guidelines given on the following pages. . . .

5) If the situation warrants, fill out a Customer Incident Form.

Aberrant Behavior: Emotionally Disturbed Persons

Emotionally disturbed persons may be suffering from mental illnesses or disorders characterized by bizarre behavior and hallucinations and may be timid and withdrawn, or violently aggressive.

Staff Procedure

1) If at any time you fear for your or the safety of others, call 9-911 immediately.

2) Arrange to have another staff member unobtrusively available as back-up support. Have a pre-arranged signal in case you need your back-up to call the Police.

3) Remain at a safe distance. *Do not* touch the person. *Do not* stare, point, laugh, or whisper.

4) Do not act overly friendly or solicitous, nor hostile or confrontational.

5) Speak calmly and respond to questions and statements matter-of-factly. Do not endorse a person's hallucinations.

6) Offer the person alternatives. For example, if a person is talking loudly to him/herself, explain the library regulations about loud talking. If the person does not stop, offer a choice: "You may speak loudly elsewhere, but if you wish to remain in the library, you must observe the rules." Repeat several times if necessary.

7) If the customer persists, obtain the support of other staff and ask the person to leave the library.

8) If the customer refuses to leave, or if you consider him/her unable to function, call the Police at 9-986-6711.

EMOTIONALLY OR MENTALLY ABERRANT BEHAVIOR

1. Use a firm, commanding voice to explain the library's rules and ask the person to desist or leave.

2. Do not corner or touch the person. Leave the person space to exit the building.

3. Get backup from co-workers.

4. Call for law enforcement help if the person will not leave.

Dealing with patrons who act or talk irrationally can be difficult. If the behavior is not disturbing to others, it should be ignored. Sometimes emotionally disturbed people are library regulars about whom the staff has information (name of the caseworker, address of sheltered living situation, etc.). Occasionally, the Branch Manager may feel that it would be more productive to call the caseworker than to involve the police. This is a Common Sense Rule situation. Provided the staff and public are not endangered, the Branch Manager should use her/his judgment in deciding whom it would be best to call for help. If, on the other hand, the unusual behavior is disruptive, then the staff must act decisively.

1. Take a firm, consistent stand and speak in a commanding voice, explaining the library's rules and that, "Your behavior is disturbing to others and inappropriate in the library."

2. However, do not corner or touch the individual. Give the patron enough room to leave the building easily without feeling threatened.

3. If necessary, keep repeating your statement about appropriate behavior over and over.

4. If you are having difficulty dealing with the individual, call for help from co-workers and (in a larger Branch) let the Person in Charge know you are having trouble.

5. If the disturbance continues and the individual will not respond or is physically threatening to him/herself, other people or staff, call law enforcement immediately.

6. Write an Incident Report for your Branch's file. If a person is injured, property is damaged, or law enforcement is called, send the Incident Report to the Central Office within 24 hours.

FIGHTS, PHYSICAL OR VERBAL

1. Tell other patrons to stand back.

2. Tell the combatants to stop immediately, or leave the library.

3. If they do not stop, call law enforcement.

One of the Library System's most famous stories about a fight between patrons involved the morning edition of the *Wall Street Journal*. A branch regular, known for his otherwise quiet and polite demeanor, became furious when another patron got to the paper first. He snatched the *Journal* out of the other man's hands, the other man snatched back, and eventually they came to blows. The Branch Manager intervened, and ordered them to desist, which fortunately they did. Eventually, they were persuaded to share. These were adults, not kindergartners.

The staff's first objective in a physical confrontation between patrons is to protect the safety of other library users and staff. This may not be easy, because other patrons may want to intervene. But if the intervener is hurt, the library could face a serious liability problem.

1. In a very firm voice, order other patrons to stand back and not intervene.

2. Try to get the attention of the combatants. Order them to stop fighting immediately, or leave.

3. Do not endanger yourself by intervening physically.

4. When the fighting stops, warn the combatants that their behavior is totally inappropriate to the library, and that if it ever occurs again, the staff will get court orders forbidding them to come in to the library.

5. Call for law enforcement assistance if the fighting does not cease, or continues outside the building. Be prepared to give the police physical descriptions of the combatants.

6. Fill out an Incident Report, and send it to the Central Office if law enforcement is called.

Treat verbal confrontations between patrons in the same way.

MISSING POSSESSIONS, STOLEN WALLETS, ETC.

1. Ask the user who reports a stolen item to retrace their steps within the building, thoroughly searching the building both inside and out.

2. If the item isn't found, urge the person to file a law enforcement report.

3. Get the name, address, and phone number of the person so that she/he can be contacted if the item turns up.

The Library System is not responsible for the personal property which patrons bring into our facilities. This not only includes purses, wallets, jackets, book bags, and lunch boxes, but the backpacks and duffles which may constitute all the worldly goods of a street person.

We encourage people to be careful of their possessions, and **not** to leave them on tables, in carrels, or otherwise unattended.

People do this anyway, of course, and consequently come to the staff to report that personal property is missing or stolen:

1. Ask the person if the item could have been misplaced or left somewhere else. If not, suggest that they retrace their steps within the building.

2. If the item is not found, suggest that the person search the building inside and out, looking in all the waste baskets, outdoor trash receptacles, landscaping areas, etc.

3. Urge the person to call law enforcement if the item is not found.

4. The staff member should take the name and telephone number of the patron and give it to the Branch Office in case the bag or other item is eventually located.

5. Write an Incident Report for your Branch's file. If a person is injured, property is damaged, or law enforcement is called, send the Incident Report to the Central Office within 24 hours.

OBSCENE PHONE CALLS

1. Hang up. Do not listen.

2. Note the date and time of the call, and give the information to your supervisor.

There are people who get a thrill out of dialing a phone number and talking obscenely to whoever answers. Libraries, and their telephone reference operations, are easy targets for this kind of harassment.

The only way to handle the behavior is to not give the caller the satisfaction of listening. Just hang up. But do log the call, because if there is a sudden surge of obscene phone calls, we may decide to ask the law enforcement to investigate.

Added Note:

If you receive an obscene phone call which is directed to you personally, in which the caller uses your name, your address, your car make or license number, or any other personal information about you, **report this immediately to your supervisor, who will call the police.**

PANHANDLERS OR SOLICITORS ON LIBRARY PROPERTY

1. If you see someone panhandling or soliciting on library property explain that it is illegal.

2. If necessary, warn the person a second time, saying you will call law enforcement.

3. If the person persists, warn a final time, and call law enforcement if necessary.

Panhandling and soliciting on library property are prohibited by the California Penal Code, #647(c).

Library property extends to the library side of the public sidewalk, and includes branch parking lots for facilities we own, but not the parking lots of leased spaces in shopping centers. Panhandling and soliciting are prohibited **inside** both owned and leased library facilities.

"Panhandling" is to accost someone and beg for something, usually money. "Soliciting" is to approach with a request or a plea. Although there are more exotic examples associated with this word, the soliciting we normally see in the library is by kids selling candy to benefit a school project, or the like.

1. If you witness a violation, explain the law to the offender.

2. If the problem persists, warn the person a second time.

3. If the person continues, warn the person a third time, explaining that you will call law enforcement if she/he does not desist. Do so if necessary.

4. Take a Polaroid picture of the violator if you can.

5. Write an Incident Report for your Branch's file. If a person is injured, property is damaged, or law enforcement is called, send the Incident Report to the Central Office within 24 hours.

PETS IN THE LIBRARY

1. Animals are not allowed in the library.

2. Seeing Eye or Hearing Dogs, or dogs clearly trained to assist disabled users, are exempted from this rule.

3. Insist that any other animals be removed immediately.

People may not bring pets of any kind into the library. This includes the lobbies of branches which have them. There are three reasons for this rule:

- animals confronting one another inside a building can get into fights which are unpleasant for everyone.

- excited animals can cause accidents and discomfort among older and younger patrons.

- many people are allergic to animal hair or animal odors.

Seeing Eye or Hearing Dogs, or dogs clearly trained to assist a disabled user, are exempt from this rule.

If someone brings in a pet:

1. Ask the person to remove the animal immediately.

2. Suggest that dogs be tied outdoors, in a place where they will not frighten children. Bicycle racks are inappropriate places.

3. If appropriate, remind the person that local ordinance requires that all dogs be leashed.

4. If the person refuses to abide by the library rule say you will call law enforcement. Do so if necessary.

5. Write an Incident Report for your Branch's file. If a person is injured, property is damaged, or law enforcement is called, send the Incident Report to the Central Office within 24 hours.

See also YOUR BRANCH'S EMERGENCY PLAN FOR INFORMATION ON ANIMAL BITES AND ANIMALS IN THE LIBRARY.

SEXUAL DEVIANTS:
BOY/GIRL WATCHERS, FLASHERS, ETC.
Yakima Valley, Washington, Regional Library
Customer Relations Manual

A. Girl/boy watchers, peekers, etc.

1. If someone is suspiciously watching or following a patron or staff member, try to get a description. Note height, coloring, age, general build and what the person is wearing. Anything you can remember may be helpful.

2. Although the offender may be gone by the time you report it, it is a good practice to tell fellow staff members what the offender looks like so they can be aware. Tell you supervisor what has occurred.

3. Many times if you confront the offender and let him/her know that he/she is being watched, it will stop him/her. To confront him/her simply ask, "Are you finding the library materials you need," or other statements to that effect.

4. If the patron persists, the Librarian-in-charge will warn the offender, if located, that the behavior is offensive, and if not stopped, the police will be called.

5. If the patron persists, call the police.

6. If the police are called, notify the Associate Director or Director immediately.

7. File incident report.

B. Flashers: These people are generally passive, not violent.

1. If this happens to a staff member:

    a. Remain calm and do not show shock or alarm at the behavior, as these people thrive on your reaction.

    b. Try to remember and write down as much of a description of the offender as possible. Note age, general build and height, coloring, clothing, etc. If the patron leaves try to get a description or license number of his/her vehicle and/or direction of travel.

    c. Immediately alert other staff members including your supervisor or the Librarian-in-charge.

    d. Call the police and give them a description and location of the incident.

    e. After you call the police, notify the Associate Director or Director immediately.

    f. If the offender is still around, the staff member who witnessed the incident should identify the person to the police and have him/her arrested. (The staff member does not have to have the offender arrested but should be encouraged to. This is a serious problem and should not be taken lightly.)

g. File incident report.

2. If this happens to a patron:

    a. Help the patron calm down. If necessary, take the patron upstairs to our staff room to provide some privacy for the patron.

    b. Determine if a physical attack has taken place.

    c. Obtain a general description and location of the incident.

    d. Call the police with this information.

    e. If the offender is still around, the patron should be encouraged to have him/her arrested, but do not force this on the patron.

    f. Offer the patron whatever additional help may be necessary. Make sure the patron has regained self-possession before leaving. In the case of children, offer to call their parents, etc.

    g. After calling the police, notify the Associate director or Director immediately.

    h. File incident report.

SEXUAL DEVIANCY REPORTS BY PATRONS

1. The staff's first obligation is to the patron who reports she/he has been sexually harassed.

2. Treat the victim with respect, sensitivity, and compassion.

3. If the victim is a child, try to find the parent.

4. Get as much information about the incident as you can.

5. Telephone law enforcement.

6. If possible, send someone to photograph the perpetrator.

1. If a library user or staff member reports that she/he has been sexually harassed by someone, be calm and sensitive toward the victim. Modified by the Common Sense Rule, follow these same procedures in dealing with **potential** cases of harassment, such as "peeping toms" or "starers."

2. Ask where the incident occurred and whether the person is still in the library. If possible, get the victim to point out the perpetrator. Get another staff person to take a Polaroid picture of him. You stay with the victim.

3. Call 911 for law enforcement help. Give your name and Branch address. Tell the Dispatcher there has been an incident of sexual harassment, and encourage the victim to speak directly to the Dispatcher.

4. If the victim is unwilling to speak to the Dispatcher, give all the information communicated by the victim:

   Location of the incident
   Description of the incident
   Description of the suspect. If the suspect has left, give the last known location and the direction of travel.

5. Follow any special instructions of the Dispatcher.

6. Get the name, address and telephone number of the victim.

7. Ask the victim to sit down in a quiet corner and write down as full and accurate a description of the suspect as possible. Concentrate on age, height, type of build, color and style of hair, clothes and any distinguishing marks or mannerisms.

8. Then ask the victim to write down exactly what happened, where it happened and what was said.

9. Encourage the victim to await the arrival of law enforcement in order to answer any further questions.

10. Write an Incident Report and send it to the Central Office within 24 hours.

Added Instructions When the Victim Is a Child

1. If a child reports to you that she/he has been sexually harassed or approached, remember you have two obligations: to meet the immediate needs of the child, and to telephone law enforcement.

2. The child may be confused, frightened, or very upset. You act calmly, seeking to reassure and comfort the child.

3. Ask the child where the incident occurred, whether the person is still in the library and if the child's parent is there.

4. Send someone to find the child's parent. You stay with the child.

5. See if you can get the child to point out the perpetrator to you, and ask another staff person to take a Polaroid picture of him.

6. Describe to the parent what has happened, and say that you are obligated to report such incidents to law enforcement, which you are going to call right now. The parent will probably be upset too. Treat the parent with calmness. Try to take the parent and child into a quiet area, such as an office.

7. Call 911 for law enforcement assistance. Give your name and Branch address, say there has been an incident of sexual harassment involving a child, and give all the information communicated by the victim, as above.

8. Get the name, address and telephone number of the child.

9. If the child's parent is not present, contact him/her by phone to report the incident. Make sure there is a way for the child to get home safely. Law enforcement can help with this.

SEXUAL HARASSMENT OF STAFF

1. *Exhibitionism [flashing]:* Walk away from the patron, and immediately call law enforcement.

2. *Following, Stalking, or Staring:* Tell the patron, "I think you are following me around [or staring at me]. It interferes with my work. Please stop it right now."

3. *Repetitive Requests for Sexually Oriented Materials or Information:* After the second request, say, "We gave you that information before. I am going to write it down for you, so you won't need to ask again."

4. *Unwelcome Requests for Dates:* Say, "No, I've told you, I will not go out with you. Please do not ask me again. If you keep bothering me, I will call the police."

These four examples are the most common ways staff are sexually harassed by patrons, but not the only ones. There are three rules to remember in handling sexual harassment:

1. Do not give the harasser the satisfaction of making you visibly upset. No matter how angry, embarrassed, or offended you are by the behavior, treat it calmly.

2. Be direct and clear in the limits you set. In cases 2, 3, and 4 above, it is important for the staff person to say what the boundaries of interaction are, and stick to them.

3. You have a right to work in a place in which you are not subjected to sexual harassment by the public or your co-workers.

Exhibitionism

People, usually men, with this sexual pathology are very rarely dangerous. The purpose of their action is to get attention for themselves. Exhibitionism is illegal, and should be treated as a crime.

1. Walk away from the perpetrator.

2. Telephone law enforcement and request assistance.

3. Immediately write a description of the perpetrator.

4. If you can, photograph the perpetrator with a Polaroid camera, or ask a co-worker to do this.

5. Fill out an Incident Report and send it to the Central Office within 24 hours.

Following, Stalking, or Staring

This harassment technique is harder to handle because it looks innocent. In fact, however, it is potentially dangerous, as the increasing number of stalking cases reported in the media attests.

1. If you notice, for the second day (second shift, or whatever), that a patron is staring at you, or following you, write it down, as well as the previous incident. Also write a description of the patron.

2. Tell your supervisor if you have one.

3. Ask a co-worker to use a Polaroid to photograph the patron.

4. Try moving to a different work station if you can.

5. If the harassing behavior continues, with your supervisor, confront the patron. Either you or your supervisor can do the talking. Use direct language, stating what you believe to be the facts, and what you want the patron to do. The object is to convey to the patron that you and your supervisor mean business; sexually harassing behavior will not be tolerated.

Staff: I think you are staring at me [or following me]. This interferes with my work. Please stop it immediately, or you will have to leave the library. Please move to another place to sit.

Patron: What? I'm not staring at you! What are you talking about?

Staff: Good. Then you won't mind moving to another place to sit. Please do that, right now.

6. If the harassing behavior continues, call for assistance from law enforcement.

7. If law enforcement is called, file an Incident Report, sending it to the Central Office within 24 hours.

Repetitive Requests for Sexually Oriented Materials or Information and Unwelcome Requests for Dates

See the summary box above. Also,

1. Make sure you report these incidents to both your supervisor and co-workers, so that other staff are alerted about the problem behavior by a patron.

SLEEPING PATRONS
Yakima Valley, Washington, Regional Library
Customer Relations Manual

A. Sleeping is not allowed in the library. Library users who simply doze off for a short period may be left alone. The library's regulation pertains to habitual sleepers or those who are noisy, sprawled out on the furniture, or generally disturbing to other patrons.

B. Discretion should be used in approaching sleeping patrons. Do not physically touch or shake them. They may possibly swing out at you as you awaken them. Be sure to approach them from the front and at an arm's distance.

C. Tell the patron to remain awake.

D. Check back after approximately ten minutes. If the patron is still sleeping, wake him/her up and tell them to leave the building.

E. If the sleeping patron is drunk, will not leave, or is physically threatening, call the police.

SMELLY PEOPLE

1. Verify that the odor is so bad that it interferes with other people's ability to use the library.

2. Look for alternatives:
   Can the complaining patron move?
   Can the smelly patron move?

3. If not, ask the smelly patron to leave and not return until she/he has bathed and washed her/his clothes.

4. Give the patron a Shelter Flyer.

This is one of the most difficult situations staff can confront, particularly in areas where street people are frequent library users. Street people do not have easy access to bathing facilities or places where they can wash their clothes. This fact is not a reason to deny them access to the library. The only reason to deny them access is if they are so smelly that other people cannot use the library.

There are other kinds of odor problems which staff must sometimes handle. One is heavy use of perfume, which can offend other people. Another is people with severe environmental allergies, who complain that the library's air or the people around them are making them ill.

If a person's odor is **so strong** that it is offensive to staff or other library users (i.e., if it interferes with other people's ability to use the library), the Branch Manager or the Person in Charge should:

1. Verify the situation for her/himself. "So strong" means that it is literally nauseating to be near the person.

2. If another person has complained, ask the complainant if they are willing to agree to back the staff should a formal (i.e. police) complaint be necessary.

   If the person is **not** willing, evaluate whether the situation is worth pursuing anyway.

   Can the complainant move?

   Can the smelly person be asked to move?

3. If in your judgment the person must be asked to leave the library, quietly and politely do so, asking the person not to return until he/she has cleaned him/herself.

EXAMPLE: "Excuse me, Sir/Ma'am. I am sorry to say that the way you smell means other people cannot use the library. So I must ask you to leave right now. You can come back as soon as you have bathed and washed your clothes. Here is a list of places where you can wash."

Give the person the Flyer listing shelters.

4. If the person objects, call law enforcement.

5. In the case of a person who smells offensive due to excessive perfume, follow the same procedures, but drop the statement about bathing and washing clothes.

6. Write an Incident Report for your Branch's file. If a person is injured, property is damaged, or law enforcement is called, send the Incident Report to the Central Office within 24 hours.

If a person complains that she/he has severe environmental allergies, the Branch Manager or Person in Charge should try to establish what can be done to mitigate the problem.

Would opening the windows help?

Can the person move?

Would a fan help (but be careful about hazardous cords)?

It is important to convey sympathy to a user troubled by environmental allergies, and to attempt to make it possible for the person to use the public library. The Branch Manager might ask the patron whether she/he would find a volunteer helpful, and link the person with the Friends Office to find one.

However, the library's basic policy always applies: no one (even an allergic person) has the right to interfere with anyone else's right to use the library. There are limits on the modifications we can make.

SMOKING

1. It is illegal to smoke anything in any public building in Santa Cruz County.

2. Say to the violator, "I'm sorry, sir, but it is illegal to smoke inside any public building in Santa Cruz County. Will you please take that outside right now to put it out, or finish it there? Thanks."

3. If the violator refuses, call law enforcement.

THEFT OF LIBRARY MATERIALS OR OTHER PROPERTY

1. If the Checkpoint system alarm goes off, say, "Excuse me sir/ma'am. I think we forgot to check out your materials. Please step back to the desk and I will take care of it."

2. Keep asking for, and charging out, library items until the alarm no longer sounds when the patron steps through.

3. If you have trouble with a patron, get staff backup.

4. If your branch does not have a Checkpoint system, and you suspect a theft attempt, approach the patron with the same courtesy. Say, "Excuse me, sir/ma'am. Did you forget to check out those items? Here, let me have them and I will do it for you. May I have your library card, please."

Naturally, stealing library materials or other property is against the law. In legal terms, it is larceny, but as usual with the law, it must be handled very carefully. If we want to accuse someone of larceny, we have to demonstrate that two elements are present at the time we catch him/her:

1. that he/she in fact has the library property, and

2. that she/he intended to steal it.

If both these elements are present, the thief can be detained and arrested. Demonstrating possession isn't difficult. Demonstrating intent is harder.

How to Prove Intent to Steal:

The most common way to demonstrate intent is to show that the thief concealed the item. However, just because you can't see it, does not legally mean it is concealed. To prove intent by concealment, the item has to be hidden in a place where it would not normally be carried.

> Library materials in a briefcase or backpack do not prove intent, because the patron could claim that she/he inadvertently scooped them up with personal papers.

> Library materials carried under clothing, or wrapped in something (like a jacket) can be used as a demonstration of intent; why would a man carry books under his shirt if he didn't intend to conceal and steal them?

Therefore, What to Do:

1. Never assume that a patron leaving the library with uncharged materials intends to steal them. Absent-mindedness or misunderstanding of library procedures are both reasonable explanations.

2. Approach people with courtesy, using non-accusatory words which objectify the situation: "Excuse me, sir/ma'am. I think we missed checking out your materials. Please step back to the desk and I will take care of it." Or, "Excuse me, sir/ma'am. Did you forget to check out those items? Here, let me have them and I will do it for you. May I have your library card, please."

3. If the patron refuses to surrender the material, say "It looks to me like you are trying to take library materials without checking them out. That is against the rules. Please give them to me." Use an authoritative tone of voice. Make it clear that you mean business. Experience tells us that this often persuades a patron to hand over the material.

4. If the patron again refuses, say the same thing again, this time adding the information that you will telephone law enforcement.

5. If the patron still refuses to surrender the material, call law enforcement. If the patron tries to leave, do not risk injury to yourself by attempting to detain him/her.

6. Immediately write down a physical description of the patron, and give this to the police when they arrive. If you know the patron's name and address (or can get it from the database), give this to the police too.

7. Fill out an Incident Report, and send it to the Central Office within 24 hours.

When the Checkpoint Alarm Keeps Sounding:

The Checkpoint System alarm is activated by only two things: "preconditioned" library materials, and electronic door opening cards which use radio devices. So if the alarm continues to sound, and you have checked out the books properly, your object is to get the patron to give up materials she/he has hidden, or produce an electronic access card which is setting off the system.

If you have checked out the materials and the alarm sounds again, say, "The Checkpoint system is not supposed to alarm for anything but library materials. Please help me find the cause of the alarm so that it can be corrected and will not happen to anyone else."

Ask the patron to walk through the system with their personal belongings, and then to go through minus each of the items (purse, briefcase, etc.).

Once the source is pinpointed, the patron will usually come up with library materials they have stashed away. Take them, thank the patron for his/her cooperation, and explain that the system is to provide better service for everyone.

If the patron does not cooperate, she/he probably is a thief. Follow procedures 4, 5, 6, and 7 above.

The Missing Barcode Scam:

Apparently some people believe that it is the barcode in an item which is the security device. He/she therefore tears out the barcode label, and walks through the Checkpoint station with the item completely visible. When the alarm sounds, she/he claims that her/his friend has already checked the item out. This is a little like telling your teacher that the puppy ate your homework.

What to Do:

1. Ask the patron for the item, and establish that the barcode has been torn out.

2. Tell the patron that you must keep the item, so that a new barcode can be put in it.

   Alas, this is all we can do here. But do be sure you get the item from the patron.

VANDALISM AND DESTRUCTIVE BEHAVIOR

1. If the patron appears to be approachable, tell him/her to stop immediately.

2. If the patron does not appear approachable, call law enforcement.

The library staff has a right and duty to protect public property. The California Education Code, Section 19910, covers this. Examples of destructive behavior are: Destroying or defacing library materials, including slicing pages from books, periodicals, and newspapers; vandalism of library property, including defacing walls and furniture, damaging facilities (such as restrooms), breaking windows, etc.

Destructive patrons can be merely careless or thoughtless, or they can be dangerous. The staff person observing the behavior must size up the situation and decide on the best method for handling it.

1. If the patron seems harmless, tell the patron to cease the behavior immediately.

SANTA CRUZ • PUBLIC
L I B R A R I E S
A City County System

INCIDENT REPORT FORM

BRANCH _____ DATE _____ TIME _____

STAFF PRESENT _____

NAME OF PATRON (if known) _____

DESCRIPTION OF INCIDENT _____

_____

_____

DESCRIPTION OF PATRON _____

_____

WITNESSES _____
(Get phone numbers and addresses if possible)

_____

ACTION TAKEN _____

POLICE/FIRE CALLED?   YES ___ NO ___ TIME _____   TIME ARRIVED _____

ADDITIONAL COMMENTS _____

INSTRUCTIONS TO STAFF HANDLING INCIDENT: Please fill out this form as completely as possible, and sign it below. Give it to your Branch Manager.

_____
Signature of Staff Person
Handling Incident

INSTRUCTIONS TO BRANCH MANAGERS: If the incident involved personal injury to a staff person or member of the public, damage to public property, or law enforment officials were called, SEND THIS FORM TO THE CENTRAL OFFICE WITHIN 24 HOURS. DO NOT KEEP A COPY. If necessary, the office staff will file appropriate risk management reports, attesting that all other records of the incident have been destroyed.

224 Church Street Santa Cruz, California 95060 • (408) 429-3533 • Fax: (408) 425-4927

EXAMPLE: [this really happened]

Staff: Sir, slicing pages out of a library magazine is destroying library property, and is against the rules. Please stop it right now.

Patron: Hey, it's just an advertisement. That's not destroying property. Anyway, I'm a taxpayer. This belongs to the taxpayers, right?

Staff: If you cut an advertisement out of a magazine you are interfering with someone else's right to read it. That is why it's considered vandalism, and is against the law.

Report the behavior to the Person in Charge, who should discuss restitution with the offender.

2. If the patron does not appear to be approachable, call law enforcement immediately. The Library will prosecute anyone who maliciously destroys library property, but arrest power can only be exercised when the vandalism has been observed and is committed in the presence of the person signing the citation or making the arrest.

3. In either case, write an Incident Report [see pages 188-189] for your Branch's file. If law enforcement is called, send the Incident Report to the Central Office within 24 hours.

VERBAL ABUSE OF STAFF

1. Remain calm, and remember to use your Angry or Irate Patron techniques, particularly "Stand and Deliver."

2. Say to the patron, "Your language and behavior are not appropriate to the library. You must either stop, or leave right now and come back when you have calmed yourself."

3. Get backup from other staff.

No staff person needs to listen to abusive or obscene language from a library user.

1. Try to remain calm, and remember that you personally are not the cause of the patron's inappropriate response or language. The patron would like to make you mad. Don't provide that satisfaction. Instead, use "Stand and Deliver" to wait the patron out.

2. Remember, too, that other patrons are listening to how you handle the situation. **They** are on your side, and will stay there if you are calm, do not get angry, and act reasonably but firmly.

3. Tell the patron, "Your language and behavior are not appropriate in the library and are causing a disturbance. You must either stop, or leave right now and come back when you have calmed yourself."

4. Other staff should come to support the staff person being abused. The Person in Charge should intervene to try to defuse the situation. Sometimes the best thing to do is just to walk away.

5. If the patron continues to be abusive, do not argue. Say, "You will have to leave the Library right now or I will call for help."

6. If the patron refuses to leave, the Person in Charge or a co-worker should call law enforcement or other community backup.

7. Write an Incident Report for your Branch's file. If a person is injured, property is damaged, or law enforcement is called, send the Incident Report to the Central Office within 24 hours.

See also ANGRY AND IRATE PATRONS

LIBRARY RULES

The public library is open to all. No one has the right to interfere with anyone else's right to use the library.

- ◆   **NO SMOKING**

- ◆   **NO FOOD OR BEVERAGES**

- ◆   **NO BICYCLES IN BUILDING**

- ◆   **NO SOLICITING OR PANHANDLING**

- ◆   **NO ANIMALS EXCEPT GUIDE DOGS**

- ◆   **PLEASE TALK IN SOFT TONES ONLY**

- ◆   **BACKPACKS AND PERSONAL BELONGINGS MUST BE KEPT UNDER TABLES OR CHAIRS**

- ◆   **CHILDREN UNDER 9 YEARS MUST BE SUPERVISED BY A PERSON 14 YEARS OF AGE OR OLDER**

- ◆   **LIBRARY MATERIALS AND FURNITURE BELONG TO ALL THE PEOPLE. PLEASE USE THEM WITH CARE**

Index